I0815285
STOP
DENALI
NATIONAL PARK
ALASKA
FLORIDA
MAP OF

GUTTED
WELCOME TO
COLORADO

Somewhere between Dan and Sam's humorous banter, courageous adventures, and insightful applications, you'll find yourself wanting to follow their lead in choosing an adventurous existence over an average one. They remind us that just because fear is a natural place to start, it doesn't mean you have to stay there. And that when you go places you've never been before, you'll have to go past where you normally stop. Get ready to stiff-arm what's comfortable and embrace the unfamiliar.

JEFFERY PORTMANN
Pastor at Gateway Church, Poulsbo, WA, and author of *Delayed Destiny*

We've known Sam since she was a preteen and Dan since he was in college. Reading this book made us not only laugh out loud at some of their shenanigans but also burst with pride at their love for God, each other, their children, and life. They are the real deal, and this book is not only entertaining (you feel like you're sitting right there with them!) but also inspirational and encouraging. It's a great read that's hard to put down. We can't wait for the sequel!

ERIC AND TRISHA PORTER
Founders of Backyard Orphans, backyardorphans.org

I laughed, I cried, and I closed the book feeling encouraged. While reading, I was on a mini adventure of my own. This book will inspire you to step outside of your comfort zone, challenge you in your faith, and make you want to take on any adventure that comes your way.

HANNAH COOK
Social media influencer

Life often presents us with unexpected twists and challenges, but Dan and Sam masterfully remind us that these moments are opportunities for growth and transformation. *Always Choose Adventure* is more than a book—it's a guide for anyone yearning to embrace the unknown, take risks, and rediscover God's purpose in their life. With relatable stories, practical wisdom, and an encouraging tone, this book will inspire readers to keep moving forward no matter what life throws their way. I wholeheartedly recommend it to anyone ready to take the leap into the extraordinary!

STONE MOSS
Founding pastor, Limitless Church

I had a front-row seat watching Sam and Dan leap from the comforts of an ordinary life into the great unknowns of a life of adventure—one where the scales of risk and rewards teeter constantly and uncertainty is the only certainty. No doubt, the "leap" cost them everything. In return, it gave them everything back, plus more. Follow their lead to find out for yourself what being fully dependent on and surrendered to God looks like as you leap into whatever adventure of a lifetime God is calling you to.

KIRK NOONAN
Leader of Convoy Nation for Convoy of Hope

This couple is dynamite! It's who they are and what they do. Dan and Sam have lived out extraordinary experiences with joy and determination even when they didn't know what would happen next. Their captivating and compelling stories will inspire you not to miss out and to embrace the unexpected with excitement!

SCOTTY AND CASEY GIBBONS
Authors, speakers, ministry leaders, and founders of realifefamily.org

Dan and Sam are such a breath of fresh air! They take away excuses and are relatable in so many ways. They are real and inspiring, and reading their family's engaging story definitely makes us want to get out there and live bigger!

MICAH AND SARAH WALLACE
Social media content creators

As a friend and fellow content creator, I cannot recommend *Always Choose Adventure* enough. Watching and now reading about Sam's journey through surrogacy is part of what gave our family the courage to proceed with surrogacy ourselves. Dan and Sam beautifully share how true adventure lies not in comfort but in embracing challenges with trust and courage. This book is a powerful call to live a life of purpose, rooted in sacrifice and faith.

SHANNON WILLARDSON
Influencer and content creator, @shannonwillardson

ALWAYS CHOOSE ADVENTURE

A Tyndale nonfiction imprint

DAN & SAM MATHEWS

WITH CAROL TRAVER

ALWAYS CHOOSE Adventure

ONE COUPLE'S JOURNEY OF
CHASING THE THINGS IN LIFE THAT MATTER MOST

Visit Tyndale online at tyndale.com.

Visit Tyndale Momentum online at tyndalemomentum.com.

Visit the authors online at wearedanandsam.com.

Tyndale, Tyndale's quill logo, *Tyndale Momentum*, and the Tyndale Momentum logo are registered trademarks of Tyndale House Ministries. Tyndale Momentum is a nonfiction imprint of Tyndale House Publishers, Carol Stream, Illinois.

Always Choose Adventure: One Couple's Journey of Chasing the Things in Life That Matter Most

Cover and interior design by Julie Chen

For information about special discounts for bulk purchases, please contact Tyndale House Publishers at csresponse@tyndale.com, or call 1-855-277-9400.

Library of Congress Cataloging-in-Publication Data

A catalog record for this book is available from the Library of Congress.

ISBN 979-8-4005-0209-5

Printed in India

31 30 29 28 27 26 25
7 6 5 4 3 2 1

This book is dedicated to our children,

Canyon and Ember.

May you always choose adventure wherever God leads you.

Contents

SEPTEMBER 2020
25 MILES NORTHEAST OF MULESHOE (YES, YOU READ THAT RIGHT), COLORADO

D: The second I popped the hood, a thick cloud of white smoke came billowing out. Fanning it away as best I could, I pulled out my phone, hit the flashlight, and started scanning the engine. What I was looking for was anyone's guess.

The truck was old, but it had been running fine—until I turned onto the exit ramp. Then all of a sudden, the power steering went out, the lights on the dash started blinking, and smoke began pouring out from under the hood. It was all I could do to get us off the highway before the truck died completely.

"Are we out of oil again?" Sam asked, appearing at my side.

I checked the dipstick. "No, the oil's fine."

"Where's all that smoke coming from?"

"It's steam. It's coming from the radiator. I'd check it, but the cap's too hot to touch."

"Do you think that's the problem?"

"Maybe."

Now, I'm not a mechanic, but I do know a couple of things, like if you run out of oil, the engine will seize up. And if you run out of coolant, the engine will overheat. When I pulled off the road, the temperature gauge was all the way up, and I could smell coolant, but that didn't explain why the power steering went out. There was one other thing I knew to check.

I angled the light toward the front of the engine until I could see the serpentine belt. I knew that if that was broken, pretty much nothing would function properly. It was a little frayed, but it looked to be in one piece. When I reached down and snagged it with my finger, though, I noticed there was a lot of slack in it.

"Oh, now I see what happened. There should be a little tensioner pulley here holding the belt in place, keeping it taut."

Sam leaned in for a closer look. "Where?"

"That's the problem. It's gone. It must have broken off somehow."

"Can you fix it?"

"Not without a new pulley."

I stepped back from the truck and looked around. We were in a gravel lot outside of what appeared to be an old boarded-up motel. I turned and looked back toward the highway, but there wasn't a single car in sight. The last major town we'd passed was a good fifty to sixty miles back, and it was starting to get a little dark. And if that wasn't ominous enough, we were right across the street from a cemetery.

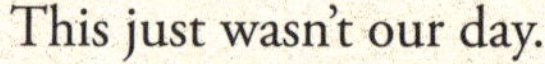

This just wasn't our day.

Heck, it wasn't even our truck. *Our* vehicle had broken down in Kansas just after breakfast. This one was a loaner.

"I mean, seriously . . ." Sam stared at the engine, shaking her head. "What are the odds of two vehicles breaking down in one day?"

She had a point.

Actually, the first one was kind of on us. We always check the tires and top off all the fluids before we go on a road trip. Why we hadn't thought to check the oil before we left Missouri that morning, I'll never know. And by *we*, I mean *me*, so . . . technically, I guess the first one was on me.

I checked my phone. "At least we still have cell service. Let me see if I can find an auto parts place somewhere around here." As I glanced around, though, I wasn't optimistic.

S: While Dan was scanning Yelp, I texted the production team to let them know we would be arriving a little later than expected.

We were on our way to Alamosa, Colorado, to compete in a new reality show where teams are given five days to turn a totally gutted vehicle into a fully functioning house on wheels. We'd been renovating RVs as a side hustle and documenting the process on Instagram for a little over a year, so when a friend forwarded us an email inquiry from the producer, we thought, *Why not?* Dan and I are always on the lookout for fun opportunities to stretch ourselves and try something new, so it felt like a perfect fit.

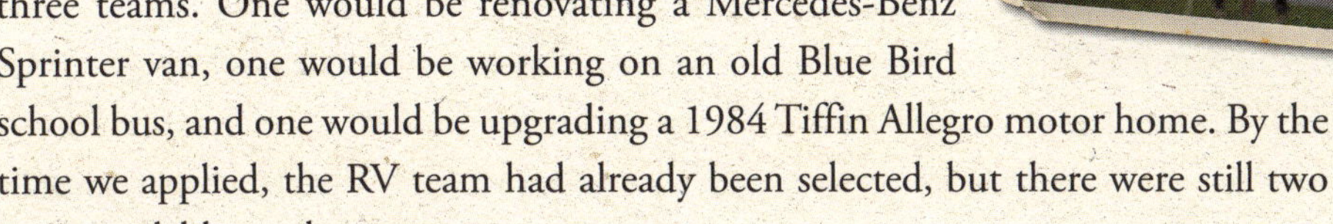

The show was called *Gutted*, and they were looking for three teams. One would be renovating a Mercedes-Benz Sprinter van, one would be working on an old Blue Bird school bus, and one would be upgrading a 1984 Tiffin Allegro motor home. By the time we applied, the RV team had already been selected, but there were still two spots available on the van team.

Now, we had zero experience doing *anything* with vans. All we knew for sure was that this would be a little harder, because with RVs, the basic plumbing and electrical work is already done. With a van, all that would have to be installed from scratch, and our forte was more in carpentry and interior design. Still, we figured it would be a great opportunity to get to know some other people in the tiny-living community, get more exposure on social media, and pick up some new skills. Plus, it sounded like a lot of fun—at least it did to us.

My mom, on the other hand, was less enthusiastic. Within minutes of texting her that Dan and I had been chosen for the show, she was on the phone lecturing me about the homicide rates in Alamosa.

"I'm just saying, Samantha, according to this website, there is a crime committed in Alamosa every five hours and twenty-five minutes. Plus, it has an overall crime grade of F, which means the chances of you becoming a victim of a violent crime there is 1 in 107. And the kidnapping rate . . ."

"Mom," I jumped in, "relax. We're gonna be fine."

Meanwhile, Dan was in the kitchen laughing to himself. *His* immediate reaction when the *Gutted* team had called was, "Awesome! That sounds like a lot of fun!" Of course, that's pretty much Dan's reaction to every wild idea that comes our way. Seriously, the guy almost bought a penguin once just because it sounded like fun.

There was a second of silence on the other end, followed by, "I'm going to need the address of this place."

"Mom, we don't even know where we're going. All we know is that it's somewhere out in the desert. We might not even have cell service."

"If you don't hear from us in seven days, Granny," Dan said with a laugh, "then get worried." Dan has always had a knack for defusing intense conversations between my mom and me. Pushing my mom's buttons is one of his favorite pastimes (the fact that she hates being called Granny is a prime example).

As usual, she was not amused. "What about the kids?"

"Justine is going to watch them."

My mom, my sister, and my grandparents all love taking care of Canyon and Ember, and we couldn't be more grateful. Dan and I both love to travel and go camping, and most of the time we bring the kids with us. Still, having family nearby gives us a chance to spend some one-on-one time together—or, in this case, to take off for a week to renovate an old van with a bunch of strangers in the desert.

"But you'll be gone a whole week, Sam."

"They'll be fine, Mom."

I knew there was nothing I could say that would make her worry less, but the truth was, this wasn't our first rodeo. Our kids were cool with us leaving from time to time. Plus, they both loved spending time with my family, and at three and five, they really didn't have much concept of time. We could be gone for one day or seven, and they wouldn't know the difference.

"But Sam—"

"Mom, seriously, we're gonna be okay. We're just going to drive out to Colorado, do the show, and come back home. What's the worst that could happen?"

"Look at the bright side, Granny," Dan joked. "Worst-case scenario, you're the sole beneficiary of our life insurance policy."

Again, she was not amused. Nor was she particularly delighted with our current situation.

I leaned against the side of the truck and, as if on cue, a text popped up from my mom. She had been tracking us on her phone and wanted to know why we had suddenly pulled off the road in the middle of nowhere—again.

"Oh, yeah." I sighed. "We are never going to hear the end of this."

"Hey!" Dan's face lit up. "There's an O'Reilly Auto Parts a couple of miles from here. Fingers crossed they've got the right parts, and someone can drive them out here."

While Dan called the store, I got back in the truck and shot my mom a quick text:

> Just a little car trouble. Nothing to worry about. Dan's on with an auto parts place right now. We should be on our way again soon.

The three little dots appeared almost instantly.

> Again?!

Before I could respond, Dan appeared at the window.

"Good news—they've got the belt, and he's checking on the pulley. But they're shorthanded tonight and can't send anyone out here, so I'm just gonna start walking."

Seriously? Not to give credence to my mother's paranoia, but the vacant lot of an abandoned motel? Across from a cemetery? In the middle of nowhere? At night? We might as well have broken down on the set of a slasher film.

I reached over and grabbed my purse. "I'm coming with you."

"No, you need to stay here."

"Why?"

"Because all our tools are in the back."

My eyes darted from the boarded-up motel to the cemetery. "Yeah, but . . ."

"You'll be fine. My pistol's in my bag. Just keep the windows up and the doors locked. I shouldn't be more than two hours, tops."

Honestly? I'd rather they stole the tools. "Dan—"

"Hold on a sec," he said, taking a step back to continue the call.

Oh, and for the record, Dan's "pistol" is actually a spring-operated prop gun that shoots marble-sized BBs. We got it as a thank-you for some promotional work we did for a nonlethal self-defense company. I'm not even sure it could break the skin.

When Dan got back in the truck, he was all smiles. "Good news, babe. Turns out there was a local mechanic in the store. He overheard our conversation, and he's gonna come out here with the parts."

I breathed a huge sigh of relief. "Thank God. Hopefully he can fix it and we can get back on the road!" I shot my mom a quick text.

Good news! A local mechanic is on his way.

Actually, it was miraculous news. We'd had two different vehicles break down on us, yet somehow we were still on track to arrive in Alamosa by nightfall. It hardly seemed possible.

A few minutes later, we noticed a set of headlights approaching from the west.

"That's gotta be him," said Dan.

But when the vehicle finally came to a stop, it wasn't a tow truck. It was a beat-up, rusted-out Chevy S-10 pickup that looked like it had been pieced together from the remnants of four or five different vehicles. Then the doors opened, and two guys stepped out. One was wearing a black sleeveless undershirt, knee-length jean shorts, and tall white socks, with a big silver chain that looped from his waistband back up into his front pocket. The other guy was dressed completely in black, with baggy pants and an untucked T-shirt with cutoff sleeves.

"Are you *sure* that's the guy?" I whispered.

D: I quietly shook my head. I was expecting someone in a mechanic's shirt with his name sewn on the breast pocket. And I was only expecting one guy. These two looked like they worked for a drug cartel, and as far as I could tell, neither of them was carrying any tools.

"Hold on to the pistol. I'm gonna get out and talk to these guys."

"Babe, are you sure?" Sam asked, grabbing hold of my sleeve.

"Well, we can't just sit here," I said. And for the record, no . . . I wasn't sure. Normally, I'm a glass-half-full kind of guy. Actually, I'm a glass-*overflowing* kind of guy. But these two dudes were seriously testing my optimism.

I walked around to the front of the truck to get a better look. The guy in the jean shorts was older, with a long, grizzly-looking gray goatee. He had a massive faded-out tattoo covering the top of his left arm, and his face, neck, and arms were completely covered in scars, as if he'd been badly burned. His right hand was frozen into a partially curved claw, and it looked like the tips of several of his fingers were missing. The other guy was younger, with a tattoo peeking out from under the collar of his shirt. Frankly, he looked like he'd done hard time. They both did.

We made eye contact, but nobody said anything. Then they took a few steps forward, the gravel from the parking lot crunching under their feet.

As I stood there in my running shorts, T-shirt, and loafers, with Sam in the truck behind me holding a glorified BB gun in her lap, it slowly washed over me: *Oh, yeah . . . we are 100 percent dead.*

Okay, maybe not 100 percent, but things had definitely gotten a little dicey.

To be continued . . .

WHAT'S THE WORST *That Could Happen?*

D & S: You might know us from our social media platforms, or you might have no idea who we are. If you've heard anything about us, you may know that the things we value most are faith, family, and adventure. In that order! On these pages, we hope that you'll come with us on the greatest adventure of all time, and it might not be what you think.

In a book about adventure, it's important to call out the elephant in the room (or the truck, as the case may be). Situations like this one are exactly why a lot of people avoid taking chances and stepping out of their comfort zone in the first place. Heck, even our own worst-case scenarios for this trip didn't include breaking down in the middle of the desert and having to fend off two ex-cons in a parking lot. But here's the thing: if you live your life constantly worrying about everything that could go wrong and avoiding risks at all costs, you're going to miss out on an awful lot.

It's like our kids with food. Our daughter, Ember, will try anything you put in front of her—hot, cold, sweet, spicy, yellow, green, orange, or purple—it doesn't matter. She doesn't always end up liking it, but she always gives it a shot. And because she's

willing to try anything Sam makes, she is forever stumbling upon her new favorite snack.

Then there's our son, Canyon. It's a battle getting him to try anything new—and we're not talking sushi or haggis here; we're talking ice cream and fruit snacks. That kid once refused to eat his favorite applesauce because the manufacturer changed the packaging. It doesn't matter what we say or do; he flat out refuses to expand his palate beyond chicken nuggets and PB&J.

The only one who has ever had luck convincing him to try something new is Ember. It's diabolical, really. He'll let her try it first to see how she reacts. If she likes it, he might give it a shot. If she makes a face or spits it out, he just glares at us accusingly, like, "See? I told you!" The weird part is that outside the dining room, that kid is a total daredevil. You can toss him into almost any outdoor situation—fishing, climbing, hiking, hunting—and he doesn't even flinch. But when it comes to fine dining, Canyon's motto is "Better safe than sorry."

The thing is, we don't believe God put us on this earth to be "safe," to eat the same thing at every meal, to do the same thing day in and day out, or to spend all our evenings and weekends camped out on the sofa watching TV or scrolling on our phones. We believe we were made to experience life—to choose adventure, to take risks, to explore, to try new things, and to discover all the beautiful and amazing places and cultures this world has to offer.

The Bible is full of examples of people who followed God's call to do things the rest of the world thought were out there—too risky, too dangerous, too out of the ordinary. Take David, for example—a shepherd boy who could have stayed safe and far from conflict while watching over his flocks. Instead, he did what literally everyone else was afraid to do: he fought a giant who looked impossible to defeat. He didn't know what the outcome would be, but he had total faith and trust in God. This ultimately led to victory for his nation. Or think about Daniel, who got thrown into the lions' den because he continued to pray to God despite the king's law against it. While everyone else was complying, he went against the norm, even at the risk of losing his life. In each case, these believers stepped out

IF YOU LIVE YOUR LIFE CONSTANTLY WORRYING ABOUT EVERYTHING THAT COULD GO WRONG AND AVOIDING RISKS AT ALL COSTS, YOU'RE GOING TO MISS OUT ON AN AWFUL LOT.

in faith and were obedient to God, helping other people and broadening their horizons along the way.

We're guessing the reason you picked up this book is because you're looking to add a bit of adventure into your life, and that's awesome!

There are plenty of obstacles to adventure. Not only will people question your choices (or even your sanity!), but you will also have to face the voice of fear and uncertainty in your own head. Like Canyon staring down a dill pickle, you might think, *What if I don't like it?* Or maybe, like Sam's mom, you can't stop wondering, *What if something bad happens?* Or the big one: *What if I fail?*

S: We know firsthand that stepping out of your comfort zone into the great unknown can be scary. Take it from the girl who once found herself clinging to a BB gun in the front seat of a broken-down truck in the middle of nowhere.

But just because something is different or unfamiliar doesn't automatically mean it's going to be bad. Most of us just have a tendency to expect the worst.

When I said, "What's the worst that could happen?" I wasn't thinking about crime rates, car crashes, criminals, cannibals, and everything else that could possibly go wrong. What I meant was that even if something *did* go wrong, it wouldn't be the end of the world.

If our car broke down, we'd get it fixed. If we couldn't fix it, we'd get a loaner. If we got lost, we'd stop and ask for directions. If we didn't win the competition, at least we'd make some new friends and have some stories to tell when we got back.

It all depends on how you look at it.

Just for fun, what if—instead of anticipating the

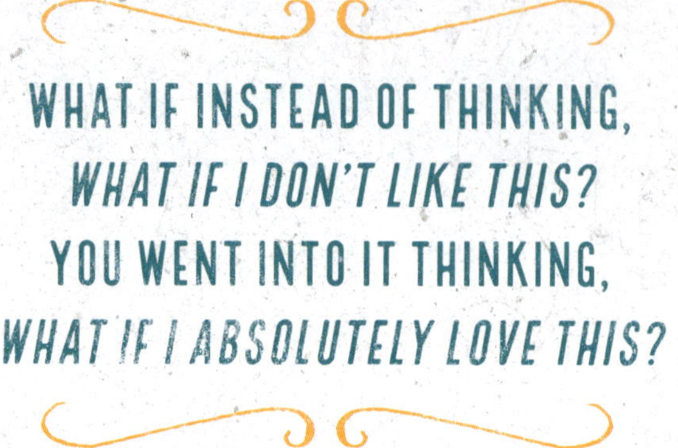

worst—you walked into each new experience the way Ember heads into a meal? In other words, what if instead of thinking, *What if I don't like this?* you went into it thinking, *What if I absolutely love this?* Instead of thinking, *What if I hate this new job?* you thought, *What if I just found my new calling?* Or, instead of thinking, *What if I fail?* you thought, *What if this ends up being the greatest experience of my life?*

That's the mindset of an adventurer! It's not about being fearless. You won't find either of us standing in line to jump off a bridge with a rubber band tied around our waists or voluntarily hurling ourselves out of a plane at 13,000 feet.

Choosing adventure isn't about being a daredevil. It's about wanting more out of life than the typical nine-to-five, being willing to step out of your comfort zone and try something new, and understanding that even if things don't turn out the way you'd hoped, there is still value in the experience. It's not necessarily about traveling or having a bold personality or not being tied down. It's also a mindset: being open to taking on new challenges, meeting new people, and saying yes to what God is calling you to do.

And anyone can do it!

Whether you look at every unexplored fork in the road as an exciting opportunity to go someplace you've never been, try something you've never done, and become friends with people you'd otherwise never meet; or you're more cautious, preferring to have every step mapped out in advance and avoid situations that push you

outside of your comfort zone—rest assured, you're invited into a life of adventure!

From the moment we said, "I do," we have been 100 percent committed to living a life of adventure. Over the past ten years, we've started multiple businesses (some of which succeeded and some of which didn't), we've traveled across the country in a house on wheels (with and without incident), we've made some smart investments (and some epically bad ones), we've taken jobs we loved (and some we hated), we've built a social media community (and we've been mercilessly skewered by trolls), we've started a family, and—through methods that might be considered unconventional—we've helped two other couples do the same. We've faced some of our greatest fears and lived to tell about it, and we've tried and succeeded and tried and failed more times than we can count. And even though things haven't always worked out the way we hoped, we wouldn't trade any of our adventures for a life of complacency, because every experience—the good, the bad, and even the downright ugly—has drawn us closer to each other and closer to God.

So, for the next ten chapters, think of us as your own personal Ember. Let us go first. We'll share some of our favorite adventures with you so you can learn from our successes and failures, and hopefully see that new experiences aren't something to be feared but something to be embraced. And Lord willing, by the time we're finished, you'll be ready to throw caution to the wind and step out into your own great unknown—whatever that might be!

After all, what's the worst that could happen?

WE WERE MADE TO

Experience Life,

Choose Adventure,

Take Risks,

Explore &

Try New Things.

1

YOU DON'T KNOW *What You're Missing*

D: I don't know about you, but for me, nothing says "adventure" like a road trip—leaving everything behind, going wherever the wind takes you, seeing new things, exploring new places. Unless, that is, you're traveling with Sam's family, in which case you drag along everything you own, every second is mapped out and accounted for, and nothing—and I mean *nothing*—is worth straying from your itinerary!

You know that expression, "Some people wouldn't know a good time from a hole in the ground?" Well, thanks to my mother-in-law's obsession with sticking to a schedule, we almost missed out on seeing the biggest hole in the ground of all time . . .

It was 2014. Sam and I had been married for a little over a year, and we were going on a road trip with her mom and sister to visit some of their extended family in Phoenix. Now, I grew up in Wisconsin with four siblings, and my dad was a long-haul trucker, so we couldn't afford to do big cross-country trips. Instead, every summer, we would hitch our little Jayco pop-up camper to the back of our minivan and drive up to Spencer Lake in Waupaca to spend a week hiking, hanging out at the beach, and swimming in the lake. It was a ton of fun, but it was still Wisconsin, so needless to say, I was super excited about finally getting to do a road trip west of Missouri.

In my head, I pictured us all in a roomy SUV, windows down, a nice cool breeze, and George Strait, Garth Brooks, and Tim McGraw playing on the radio.

What I got was the four of us crammed into a tiny four-door sedan that Sam's mom, Robin, had rented from Avis, and Sam and her sister in the back seat singing along to the Backstreet Boys and Britney Spears.

S: If I may interject for a minute here . . . I love Dan, but there was no way we were going to drive fourteen hundred miles listening to songs about dogs that ran away from home, guys that just got dumped, or some dude going on and on about a tractor.

D: I'm sorry, babe, you're right. Fourteen hundred miles of cheesy boy bands singing about high school relationships is *much* better. I don't know what I was thinking.

Also, I'm not what you'd call a neat freak, but when I'm on a road trip, I like the vehicle to be organized. I can't stand it when I go to rest my arm on the center console or the back of the seat next to me only to end up knocking someone's purse onto the floor, sticking my elbow in somebody's ice cream, or spilling someone's coffee all over the place. I'm telling you, that little sedan was packed from floor to ceiling with duffel bags, blankets, pillows, water bottles, an entire grocery bag filled with snacks, and a whole bunch of other stuff we didn't need. It was like traveling cross-country in a storage unit.

S: Okay, I'll concede that the car was a little cramped. My mom has always been a rainy-day packer. And to a certain extent, I get that. I mean, you never know what you're going to need, so as long as there's room, why not bring it along?

D: Yeah, but in this case, there really wasn't room.

S: All right, I'll give you that one too. Mom always rents the smallest car possible because it's cheaper, so in addition to putting bags in the trunk, we also end up cramming them against the back dash and along the floor of the back seat. There's barely anyplace to put your feet. You just have to roll with it—it's all part of the experience.

D: I'm just saying, you could have had a little more legroom if the three of you hadn't each brought your own personal blow-dryer and curling iron. Seriously, why couldn't you just share one?

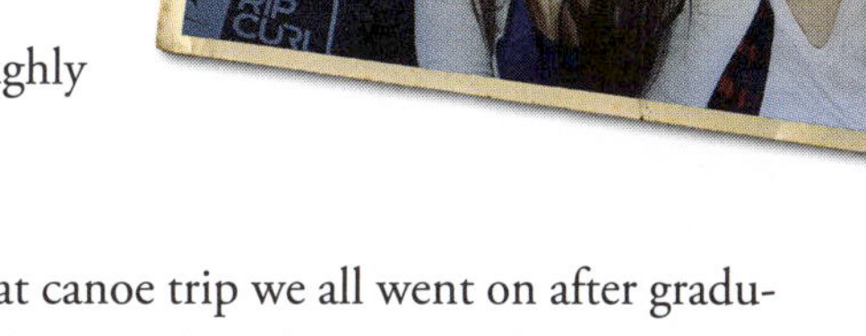

S: Because I like mine.

D: By the way, stay tuned for Sam's thoroughly enlightened chapter on downsizing.

S: Hey, mock if you will, but remember that canoe trip we all went on after graduation when Justine hit a patch of rapids and capsized, and everyone else got soaked trying to help? Who had the foresight to bring a bunch of extra clothes along?

D: I forgot about that. By the time I got Sam's sister and her friend safely to shore, Sam was already wearing a dry outfit and was passing out extra clothes like Oprah. "You get a shirt, and *you* get a shirt!"

S: If memory serves me correctly, you got a dry shirt too.

D: Regardless, they've got the car loaded up like the Beverly Hillbillies, and it's cold out, so the windows are rolled up, trapping the stench of leftover fast food like a noxious gas. The boy bands are blaring, and Sam and her sister are in the back seat doing some kind of freestyle rap (which, if I'm being honest, sounded like they were reading out loud from a Dr. Seuss book). Meanwhile Sam's mom is checking the clock on the dashboard every ten minutes to make sure we're still on schedule, because heaven forbid, we arrive at our next checkpoint fifteen minutes late.

THERE'S NO RIGHT OR WRONG WAY TO CHOOSE ADVENTURE.

By the way, when my parents used to take us to Spencer Lake, if you had to go to the bathroom, you just held it until we stopped to get gas, arrived at the campground, or made it home. But on this trip, we were constantly pulling over for restroom breaks, to grab a snack, or so someone could get out and stretch their legs for a minute even though we'd just stopped for gas ten miles back.

S: Again, it's all part of the experience, babe.

D: Needless to say, twenty hours and twelve hundred miles in, I felt like a guy in a dead-end job heading into the sixty-fifth hour of his workweek. On the upside, I'd finally convinced Sam's mom to let me drive for a while, so at least we could finally go more than one mile per hour *under* the speed limit.

Anyway, we'd just passed Flagstaff and were coming up on the turnoff to Phoenix when I saw a huge sign that read "Grand Canyon National Park, 79 miles." I'm telling you, my face lit up like a kid on Christmas morning. I sat bolt upright, pointed at the sign, and said, "Oh my gosh, you guys—look! The Grand Canyon! We *have* to go see that!"

To which Sam's mom flatly replied, "No."

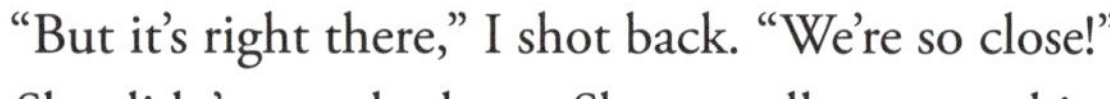

"But it's right there," I shot back. "We're so close!"

She didn't even look up. She was all cocooned in blankets, with her head nestled in a pillow that was wedged against the window.

"No, Dan," she said, stifling a yawn. "It would take us two hours just to get there. Phoenix is still four hours away, it's almost one o'clock now, and I told Seany and Diana we'd be at their house by five for dinner. She's making skirt steak."

I looked at Sam in the rearview mirror, fully expecting her to jump to my defense, but she just settled back in her seat. "For real, we've been cooped up in this car for twenty hours. We're almost there. Let's just get to Phoenix."

Believe me, nobody wanted to get out of that car more than I did, but we were within one hundred miles of one of the most spectacular natural attractions in the world! How could we *not* stop?

"Oh, come on," I all but begged. "I've never seen it before."

Sam nonchalantly replied, "Well, neither have we, but—"

"Wait a minute," I broke in, eyes wide. "You've never been there?" I just assumed they didn't want to stop because they'd already been there a half dozen times. I looked at Sam's mom. "How many times have you guys made this trip?"

"Oh, I don't know," she said. "Every year since the girls were little, so ten, maybe twelve times?"

I was floored. In my mind it would have made worlds more sense to plan a trip to the Grand Canyon and—if we had time—stop in and see Sam's family on the way. This felt entirely backwards to me. "You're telling me you've been making this trip every year for the past twelve years to see the exact same people over and over again, and you haven't stopped to see the Grand Canyon once?"

My eyes darted from Sam's mom beside me to Sam in the rearview mirror. When Sam just stared blankly at me, I looked over at Justine. She has always been more of a free spirit. She'd even been skydiving (which even *I* would never do). If anyone was going to take my side in this, I figured it would be her, so I shot her my most pathetic puppy-dog eyes, and . . .

"It *would* be kind of cool to see it," she admitted.

"Well, that's it, then," I announced. "We're going!" Heck, even if Justine *hadn't* bitten, as long as I was driving, we were 100 percent going.

As soon as I turned onto the exit ramp, I was treated to a round of spirited grumbling from Sam's mom, who emerged from her cocoon just long enough to check her map and see how much this little excursion would delay us and to call

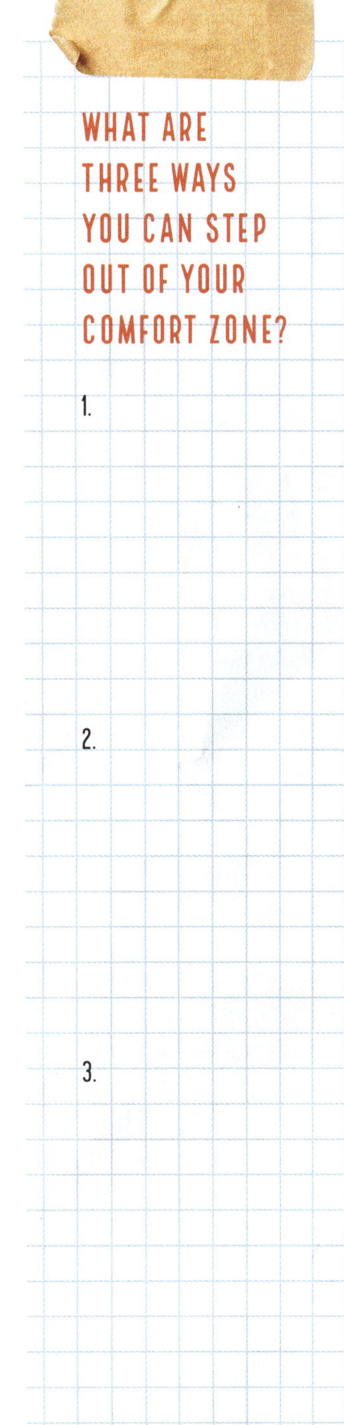

Seany and Diana to let them know we'd be arriving late because—and I quote—"Dan is *making* us go to the Grand Canyon."

She could grumble all she wanted—there was no way I was going to miss the opportunity to see something that cool just so we could get to Sam's aunt's house before the steak got cold.

For the record, Seany and Diana were both on my side.

One Way (or Another)

D: As far as I'm concerned, chucking the schedule to stop and see something really cool you didn't even know was there is the whole point of a road trip! But then, I've always loved a good adventure.

When I was a kid, my brother and I loved to take off on our bikes and go exploring in the woods by our house. We lived across the road from the Buffalo River State Trail, a thirty-six-mile trail built on an old railroad corridor that my brother and I "discovered" in elementary school. Every day, as soon as school let out, we'd take off on an excursion. Sometimes we'd pretend we were pioneers and pick wild raspberries and blackberries "to keep the settlement from starving and turning to cannibalism during the long, hard winter." Or we would run around with our BB guns playing "Wild West" or World War II, shooting at enemy trees and taking imaginary prisoners of war. And sometimes we'd ditch our bikes on the side of the path and spend the afternoon climbing trees, building forts out of fallen branches, fishing, or catching crawdads and tadpoles in the rivers and streams. We were like Huck Finn and Tom Sawyer. If we weren't climbing something, we were building something, cutting something down, or blowing something up. It was completely unscripted, and we loved it.

We went to the same family camp in Wisconsin every year, and we always had a blast. We brought our bikes, our bathing suits, and a couple of T-shirts, but that was it—no cell phones, iPods, or video games. It was all about spending time in nature. We'd play hide-and-seek in the woods, swim at the lake, and go on daily expeditions with whoever we could wrangle together at the campground. There was no schedule and no agenda. We'd take off right after breakfast and play all day with little to no adult supervision. The only rule was that if we wanted a hot dinner, we had to be back by dusk. Needless to say, we ate a lot of cold dinners, but we had the time of our lives.

S: For the record, my childhood was every bit as adventurous as Dan's—it just looked a little different. My mom and dad divorced when my sister and I were really young, so it was just the three of us girls. Still, it was important to my mom that we spend time together, so every summer she would take Justine and me camping.

When we went camping, we'd pack everything—the dog, the kennel, most of what was in our closets, all our hair stuff and makeup—you name it, we brought it! Justine and I even brought our pet hermit crabs to California with us one year. Granted, they almost died when we accidentally left them in the car in the 105-degree Texas heat, but they made it!

And of course, Mom had everything planned down to the minute. We always knew exactly which campsite we were going to, how we were going to get there, what time we were going to check in, what time we were going to eat . . .

D: That's not a camping trip, babe, that's the Marine Corps.

S: Yeah, but in Mom's defense, as a single parent, she had a lot on her plate. Plus, money was always tight, and it wasn't easy for her to take time off work. Frankly, I give her mad props for even making the effort. It would have been way easier to just drop us off at the mall for the afternoon or take us to the movies once a month. But Mom wanted us to spend quality time together as a family—and we did! It was just a little more structured—and civilized—than what Dan was used to.

D: I remember once, early in our relationship, Sam's mom said, "Hey, for Memorial Day, let's all go camping. It'll be awesome!" I figured we'd camp under the stars, cook over an open fire, go for a couple of hikes, and maybe even do a little fishing. Instead, she got us an air-conditioned cabin at KOA, cooked chicken breasts on the grill, and booked all of us manicures in town. I opted for a facial instead because it seemed more manly somehow (I was dead wrong about that, by the way). Who does that?

S: Well, pardon us for practicing good self-care. When *you* go camping, you just throw a change of socks and an extra pair of underwear in a backpack and wander into the woods with nothing but a granola bar and a sleeping bag. Who does *that*?

Anyway, because it was just the three of us, safety was also a top priority—hence the highly detailed itineraries. Whenever we went anywhere, Mom always made sure someone in the family knew exactly where we were going and when we were going to be there. To this day, whenever Dan and I travel, she still tracks us on her phone.

D: Oh, yeah, it never causes problems at all, especially when the cell coverage is spotty and messes with the GPS. There's nothing like barreling down the interstate and getting a frantic call from your mother-in-law, saying, "Why are you in a field not moving?"

S: She just likes to know where everyone is and that we're all okay.

Mock if you will, but when you're a single mom with two young girls, you do

CHOOSING ADVENTURE ISN'T ABOUT THE *HOW*— IT'S ABOUT THE *WHAT*.

what you have to do to make sure everyone's safe. What's ironic is that for all her obsession over safety, whenever we'd make the trek to California, instead of paying for a motel, Mom would just pull into a truck stop, lock the doors, and tuck blankets into the windows, and we'd sleep in the car. We did that for years until a friend pointed out that might not be the safest option for three women traveling alone. That's how we finally lucked out and started staying at the Econo Lodge in Amarillo.

D: By the way, Sam and I stayed at that Econo Lodge a few years ago, and I can honestly say they were safer sleeping at the truck stop.

S: See? My mom *is* adventurous! And for the record, we did stop along the way to see different roadside attractions. For example, just outside of Flagstaff, there's this place where a meteor hit and left a huge crater in the ground. And there's a spot in Texas called Cadillac Ranch, where there are a bunch of Cadillacs standing upright in the dirt like Stonehenge. We stopped at both of those places. And every trip, without fail, we'd stop in Groom, Texas, to see the 190-foot-tall cross just off of Route 66.

My mom wasn't opposed to doing fun, different, or exciting things. She just liked to have it all planned out. That doesn't make it wrong or any less adventurous. The important thing is, we had a lot of fun. We loved visiting our relatives, and frankly, as a kid, any time you get to drive cross-country, stay at a hotel, or eat at a restaurant, it's an adventure for no reason other than it's a break from the norm. And you know what? *That's* the whole point.

It doesn't matter whether you map out every step or fly by the seat of your pants; choosing adventure is about stepping out of your comfort zone and trying something new. There's no right or wrong way to do it. Some people like to have more of a safety net, and that's okay! Just because you have a net doesn't make walking on a tightrope any less adventurous. Choosing adventure isn't about the *how*—it's about the *what*.

All or Nothing?

D: For me, adventure is all about spontaneity—heading off into the mountains or the woods without a plan and seeing what happens. In fact, I always joke with my buddies that it's not really an adventure until something goes sideways—you make a wrong turn and lose the trail, a thunderstorm comes out of nowhere and threatens to swamp your tent, the boat springs a leak, or you're just about to pull a fish out of a hole in the middle of a frozen lake and you hear the ice start to crack.

S: Wow . . . death wish much, babe?

D: I'm just saying that for me, the whole point of an adventure is stepping out of your comfort zone and tackling things that are unfamiliar. And that's going to look different for everybody. What's comfortable for me might be a massive stretch for somebody else, and what someone else might consider par for the course could be downright unthinkable for me. For example, I feel at ease spending days on end all alone out in the wilderness, yet when I was in my twenties, I was absolutely terrified of flying, so just getting on a plane was a massive feat for me.

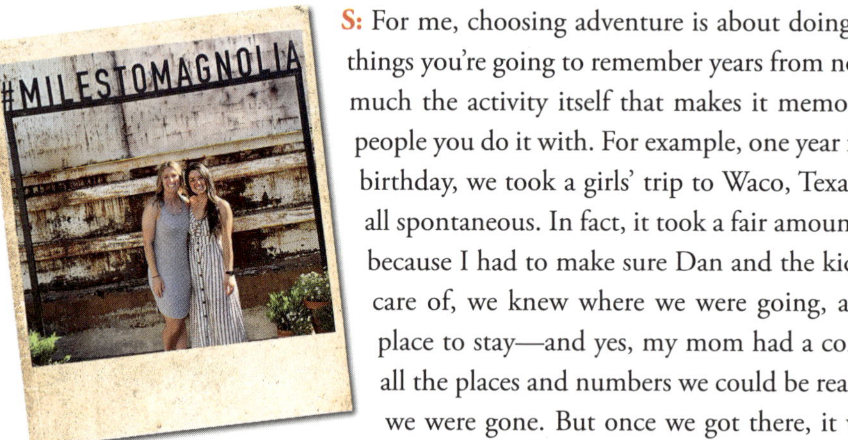

S: For me, choosing adventure is about doing the kinds of things you're going to remember years from now. It's not so much the activity itself that makes it memorable but the people you do it with. For example, one year for my sister's birthday, we took a girls' trip to Waco, Texas. It wasn't at all spontaneous. In fact, it took a fair amount of planning because I had to make sure Dan and the kids were taken care of, we knew where we were going, and we had a place to stay—and yes, my mom had a complete list of all the places and numbers we could be reached at while we were gone. But once we got there, it was the most relaxed and carefree I'd felt in years. Not only did I get to spend some quality time with my sister, but as a mom of two, I enjoyed having a little time to myself without somebody tugging on my shirt saying, "I'm hungry" every five seconds.

We took our time and walked around the Silos, visited the little shops at the Magnolia Market, had a lunch consisting entirely of cupcakes, and then changed into our swimsuits and lay out in the sun by the hotel's rooftop pool. We didn't do anything death-defying; we just relaxed and enjoyed each other's company. In fact, of all the activities we did that weekend, I think my favorite was sitting at a picnic table in the shade, enjoying a long, uninterrupted conversation with my sister. That's what choosing adventure looks like for me—getting away for a couple of days, enjoying different scenery, being relieved of some of my usual responsibilities, and not having to worry about a to-do list.

D: That's a great point. So often, the daily routine *is* our comfort zone. It's easy to get stuck on the never-ending treadmill of eating breakfast, commuting, working, making dinner, doing chores, and going to bed that, after a while, we're not living life so much as just existing. Choosing adventure is about giving yourself permission to break from the norm and do something fun every once in a while.

For us, our faith is a big part of what fuels our sense of adventure. We serve a big God who does things beyond what we can think or imagine, and he regularly calls people to step out of their comfort zone to do things like stand up to evil kings, fight giants, or face imprisonment for sharing their faith.

But like Sam said, adventure doesn't have to be death-defying. It could be something as simple as going out of your way to talk to your neighbors or taking a different route home from work one evening and exploring a new area. It might be finally trying that little restaurant you're always driving past, or, if money is tight,

packing a lunch and heading down to the river or the park to have a picnic. When we were dating, we spent a day exploring a local park. We brought some art supplies with us and painted portraits of each other, and we ate our lunch on top of a boulder near the edge of the pond. It may not have been something you'd see on a reality show, but it was a blast!

S: Oh my gosh, we had the best time! I think there's a misconception that adventure has to be a big, elaborate production. But you don't have to climb K2, go on an African safari, or backpack across Europe. You just have to do *something*.

D: Exactly. Instead of thinking of adventure as an all-or-nothing, once-in-a-lifetime proposition, it helps to get in the mindset of just trying something new once a week. Go for a walk after dinner. Eat lunch with someone you don't know at work. Stay for coffee hour after church. Turn off the TV and play a board game with your kids. Wander around your local nursery and look at the flowers. Visit your local library. Take the kids to the community pool or spend an afternoon at the zoo.

And keep an open mind. Early in our marriage, our friends invited us to spend the weekend with them in St. Louis. When I asked what was on the agenda, they said they wanted to take us to a museum. As an avid outdoorsman, I didn't exactly think an afternoon at a stuffy museum sounded like a good time, and I almost begged out of it. Thank goodness I didn't! It turns out, the City Museum in St. Louis is actually a multistory indoor playground for adults, complete with slides that go from floor to floor, secret passageways, and giant hamster tubes hovering over the ground. Had I stayed home, I would have missed out on a fun, memory-making experience. And it was right there in our own backyard!

Speaking of which . . .

The World Just beyond Your Door

D: When I was in Bible college, a couple of my buddies and I spent a summer in Long Island clearing out a pair of properties for a professor who was looking to resell them. The properties belonged to his family, and both his parents and his grandparents had some hoarding tendencies, so the houses were packed from floor to ceiling with garbage. We're talking years' worth of old newspapers, boxes filled with empty bottles and mayonnaise jars, and who knows how many cans of cat food. Both houses reeked of filth and mothballs. The yards were a complete mess too—totally overgrown and full of weeds, trash, and debris. We spent the whole summer cutting down trees, pulling weeds, mowing, throwing stuff away, fumigating, and repainting. By the time we were finished, we'd filled five industrial-sized dumpsters to the brim.

One night we went to a barbecue at a neighbor's house, and I mentioned to one of the guys there that I'd never been to New York before.

"I had no idea how wild the city was," I said. "The other night, we heard gunshots and saw a police helicopter searching the neighboring yards with a giant spotlight."

After apologizing for this less-than-favorable first impression of New York, he said, "Still, it's cool that you're getting to come out here, because there are a lot of people around here that never leave the area."

"I get that," I said, "My family travels a little bit to go camping and hunting and fishing, but for the most part, we stay pretty close to Wisconsin."

CHOOSING ADVENTURE IS ABOUT GIVING YOURSELF PERMISSION TO BREAK FROM THE NORM EVERY ONCE IN A WHILE.

He stared at me blankly for a second, then said, "No, I mean there are people here who have literally never left this neighborhood. They were born here, they went to school here, they work here, and they'll probably die here."

"You mean they've never even been to the Empire State Building or the Statue of Liberty or Times Square?"

He shook his head. "Nope. Never been to the beach or seen the ocean."

"But that's only ten miles from here."

He shook his head again. "Nope. They've never seen it."

I couldn't imagine living miles away from Manhattan, Central Park, Yankee Stadium, and the Atlantic Ocean and never seeing any of them.

That's why I was so adamant about going to the Grand Canyon. To have something that amazing right there and not go felt like a crime.

Ain't It Grand?

D: When we finally got to the canyon overlook, I was so excited I barely remembered to put the car in park before jumping out and running to the guardrail. As soon as I saw the scene, my jaw dropped, and I almost started to cry. It was absolutely breathtaking—and worth every extra second we spent in the car to get there.

S: Dan's right. It really was beautiful, and I can't believe we almost missed out on seeing it—or that, in ten years of driving to Arizona, it hadn't occurred to us to stop. I think we'd made the trek so many times that we were on autopilot—spend the night here, leave at X o'clock, turn off at exit 195, be at Aunt Diana's house by five . . .

D: And that's the problem. Too often we find ourselves walking around on autopilot, with our course locked in, and it doesn't occur to us that we *can* deviate from it.

Well, guess what? We can. And we should.

We weren't at the Grand Canyon long—maybe forty-five minutes, an hour tops. We stood at the edge and took some pictures. I even convinced Sam to take a picture with me as I dangled my feet precariously over the rim.

S: My mom was a nervous wreck when you did that, by the way.

D: I know—that's what made it so much fun. Anyway, after sufficiently frightening Sam's mom, we all piled back into the storage unit on wheels and made the final four-hour trek to Sam's aunt and uncle's house. But that little detour was the most memorable part of the trip.

Now, whenever we go on road trips, Sam is the first to say, "Hey, babe, I saw a picture of an awesome beach in Oregon, and it's only nine hours out of our way. We've got to go see it!" And I'm like, "Seriously? We're gonna drive nine hours to see a beach?" Or, "You want us to drive twelve hours out of our way to walk across some bridge in South Carolina that you read about in a book?"

You bet we do! And we've never once regretted it.

Adventure

DOESN'T HAVE TO BE

All or Nothing;

IT'S ABOUT STEPPING OUT

OF YOUR COMFORT ZONE

AND TRYING SOMETHING

New.

WHAT KIND OF *Adventurer* ARE YOU?

1. What motivates you to try something new?
   a. curiosity and the thrill of the unknown
   b. the chance to help others and meet new people
   c. the opportunity to learn new things
   d. the chance to change a typical routine, though you're more of a homebody
   e. the excitement of physical challenge and personal growth

2. Where are you most likely to take a trip?
   a. a new country, a theme park, or somewhere with multiple options for activities
   b. a nearby town or a drivable destination
   c. a cabin in the woods or someplace off the beaten path
   d. someplace local
   e. a national park or nature reserve

3. How do you like to travel?
   a. on a road trip with friends
   b. on foot, finding your own path
   c. on a guided tour or with an itinerary
   d. on clearly marked roads in a familiar area
   e. on a backpacking or off-roading trip

4. When something unexpected happens, you . . .
   a. think on your feet and adapt
   b. try to find a solution that works for everyone
   c. stay calm and assess the situation
   d. lean on others for help
   e. act quickly and decisively

5. How do you prepare for a trip?
   a. by collecting supplies and planning for situations that may arise
   b. by getting recommendations and tips from friends
   c. by reviewing maps, books, and online travel guides
   d. by making lists and doing research, research, research
   e. by doing physical training and testing your equipment

6. What's your favorite part of an adventure?
   a. discovering hidden gems, trying new foods, and finding fun photo opportunities
   b. being involved in humanitarian efforts and meeting new people
   c. going to new places, learning about historical events, and visiting museums
   d. feeling a sense of satisfaction that you accomplished something
   e. beating physical challenges and testing your limits

7. What prevents you from trying new things?
   a. lack of time and wanting to try everything
   b. worrying about how it will affect those around you and your ability to fulfill your responsibilities
   c. not feeling prepared or feeling like you lack the necessary knowledge
   d. resistance to stepping out of your comfort zone, routines, and familiar surroundings
   e. fear of failure

RESULTS

Mostly As: **THE EXPLORER.** You're driven by curiosity and the thrill of discovering something new. You thrive in the unexpected and are always ready to face a new challenge head-on. Your adventures are often filled with excitement and surprise.

Mostly Bs: **THE HELPER.** You're driven by wanting to help others and make a difference. You lead well, bringing people together to solve problems as a team. Your adventures are full of compassion and kindness.

Mostly Cs: **THE LEARNER.** You prefer adventure that is organized. You love learning and uncovering hidden information. You like reading books, maps, and stories to help with your journey.

Mostly Ds: **THE ROOKIE.** You have a mixture of excitement and anxiety, feeling hesitant to step out of your comfort zone and explore the unknown. Despite your nerves, a flicker of curiosity drives you to confront your fears. As you do, you find confidence and joy in each new experience.

Mostly Es: **THE THRILL SEEKER.** You are driven by physical challenges and opportunities to push your limits. Whether it's scaling mountains or navigating treacherous landscapes, you thrive on testing your skills and endurance. Your adventures are intense and action-packed.

If none of these fit your adventure personality, that's okay! Everyone starts somewhere, and like we always say, adventure is what you make it.

THE KEY IS TO HAVE FUN!

2

DON'T WAIT FOR *The Perfect Moment*

S: Given that this book is all about adventure, I'd love to say that Dan and I met while blind-rappelling down the sheer face of El Capitan or free diving in the Great Barrier Reef. But if you must know, we met at a bar. To be more specific, a smoothie bar. At church. Yep . . . we were wild ones.

Dan had just moved to Missouri to do a master's commission program, which is basically a one-year discipleship program connected to our church. As it happened, my sister, Justine, was also in the master's commission program, and I found myself hanging out with her and her friends, whether they were playing Putt-Putt or going to an event at our church. Our church, by the way, was huge—it had a separate building for youth, an in-house weekday preschool program, and a fitness center complete with a weight room, basketball court, and dozens of treadmills, ellipticals, and exercise bikes.

As a college student who needed flexible hours and extra downtime to study, I got myself a job working at the fitness center, greeting people as they came in and making protein shakes at the smoothie bar.

Now, despite the fact that Dan could put away five double cheeseburgers, a large

GOD KNEW WE WOULD BE BETTER TOGETHER THAN WE WOULD BE ALONE.

order of fries, and a supersized Coke in one sitting, he had a killer six-pack and about an ounce of fat on his body because (a) he had one of those magical twenty-year-old-college-kid metabolisms that I would die for, and (b) he was at the gym five days a week. After every workout, he would belly up to the bar to get a protein shake, and we would talk for hours.

D: Sam's cookie monster shakes were awesome—double peanut butter, double Oreos, 40 grams of protein, 43 carbs, 9 grams of fat, and only 380 calories (give or take, depending on how much extra peanut butter she added in "on the house"). Anyway, several hundred dollars' worth of protein shakes later, I finally said, "I'm just curious. I kind of have feelings for you. Do you feel anything on your end?"

To which she replied, "Uh . . ."

Yeah, not a great start.

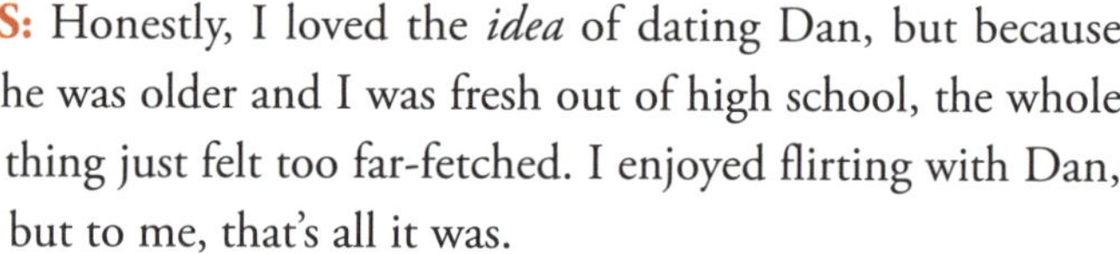

S: Honestly, I loved the *idea* of dating Dan, but because he was older and I was fresh out of high school, the whole thing just felt too far-fetched. I enjoyed flirting with Dan, but to me, that's all it was.

D: I kind of blame myself. I wasn't assertive enough, which probably sent Sam some mixed signals. I mean, for all Sam knew, I just *really* had a thing for protein shakes, and since we were usually the only two there, who else would I talk to?

S: Exactly. I was also too insecure to believe that someone like Dan would be interested in me, so instead of taking a chance, I said, "I don't really see anything between us, but I enjoy talking with you."

D: Well, I can take a hint. So a couple of months went by, during which time I saved a small fortune on protein shakes and—unbeknownst to me—Sam became interested in someone else.

One night I was at the church late cleaning one of the Sunday school rooms, and I noticed Sam was working. Since it had been a while since we talked, I went over and struck up a conversation. Before I knew it, I was stopping at the counter to get a protein shake and talk to her every day after working out again. One day, while I was drinking a smoothie, she started telling me about this guy she really likes.

S: It was kind of weird. The more I talked about how amazing this guy was and how he made me feel, the more excited Dan seemed to get. His eyes just lit up, and he couldn't stop smiling. So I was thinking, *Aw, how sweet. Look how happy he is for me!*

D: I *was* happy—because like a lovesick puppy, I thought she was being all flirty and passive-aggressively talking about me! So, in the middle of Sam's heartfelt story about this other guy, I blurted out, "Hey, I really like you too!"

She replied, "Oh, I'm so sorry. I was talking about someone else."

(Insert awkward pause here.)

S: Sorry, babe. Anyway, flash forward a couple of weeks. The other guy and I didn't work out, and I found myself thinking more and more about Dan. So I figured it was time to take a chance, and I shot him a text:

> So . . . remember how I said I didn't see anything between us . . . Well, I kinda do.

And the rest is history.

D: And it only took nine months and about $700 worth of protein shakes.

S: The thing is, it didn't have to . . .

It's Not You, It's Me

D & S: One of the main reasons people avoid stepping out and trying something new is because they're afraid of getting hurt. And we're not just talking about physical or financial safety. Telling somebody you're interested in them, asking someone out, even making new friends can be every bit as unnerving as strapping on water skis for the first time or investing in the stock market.

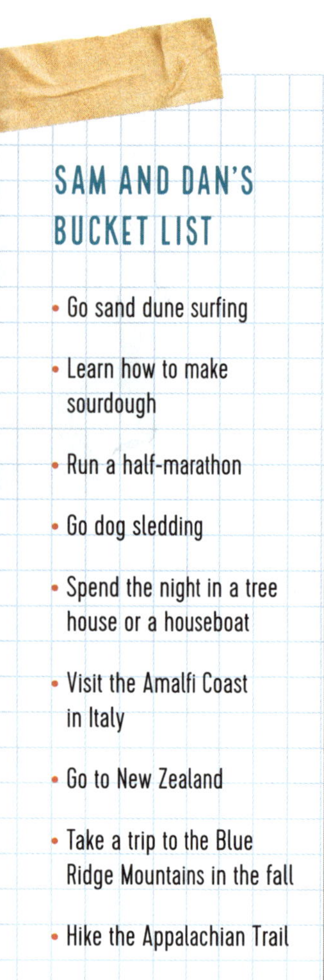

S: Putting your heart out there leaves you in a position of incredible vulnerability. What if your feelings aren't reciprocated? What if they are but not at the same level of intensity? What if, like Dan, it turns out you've completely misread the situation? Or what if the person just flat out rejects you?

D: Honestly, sometimes it feels safer and easier just to be alone. The problem is, we weren't made to be alone. In fact, in the very first book of the Bible, right after he created Adam, God said, "It's not good for the Man to be alone; I'll make him a helper, a companion." God knew we would be better together than we would be alone. This doesn't just apply to dating relationships and marriage; it's also about friendship and community. And it's true—studies show that people with strong relationships not only have lower rates of anxiety and depression but actually have higher self-esteem. There's even evidence that maintaining healthy relationships can strengthen our immune systems, help us recover from diseases faster, and even contribute to our living longer!

God designed us to be connected to others; we're not intended to live in isolation, cut off from other people. Still, there aren't many things in this world more intimidating than opening up to someone else. That's because deep down, we're all a little insecure. It's human nature to compare ourselves with other people, and more often than not, we come up short. No matter how hard we try, someone else out there seems to be smarter, prettier, richer, funnier, or more successful than we are—and therefore, more deserving of other people's love or attention.

S: Look at me. Even though Dan flat out said he was interested in me, I wouldn't let myself believe it. After all, not only was he older than me, but he was also a great-looking guy with a terrific sense of humor. He could have had his pick of any of the girls at our church. I was just some goofy kid tagging along with her big sister's friends.

D: You did make a mean protein shake, though, babe.

S: What can I say? Blended beverages are my love language. Still, if Dan had given up after that first rejection, who knows where we'd be today.

D: Yeah . . . but you also turned me down the second time.

S: True, but it was the *second* ask that gave me the confidence to finally tell you I had feelings for you too.

D: Over a month later.

S: Whatever. The point is, I almost missed out on the greatest relationship of my life because I was too frightened and insecure to put myself out there.

D: And because I was afraid of coming on too strong, I almost lost Sam to another guy.

THE GREATEST RISK LIES IN NEVER TAKING A CHANCE AT ALL— ESPECIALLY WHEN IT COMES TO TELLING PEOPLE YOU CARE ABOUT THEM.

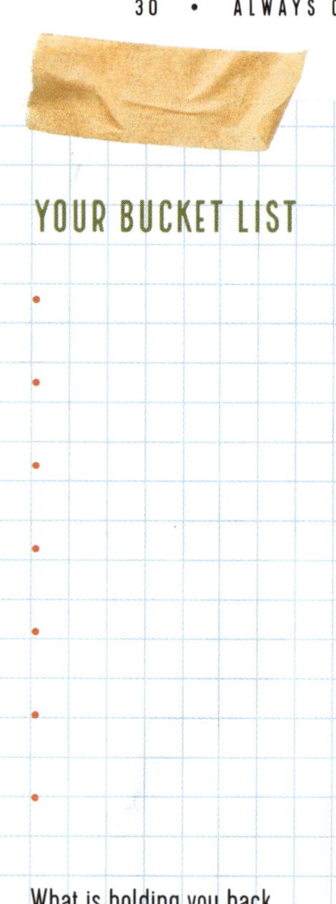

What is holding you back from these adventures? (*Money? Family? Work? Responsibilities? Time? Perfectionism? Fear?*)

S: Oh, believe me, you didn't. I only went out with that guy twice. But I couldn't stop thinking about you. We just got along so well—I couldn't imagine not being able to talk with you every day. That's why I decided it was worth taking a chance. It's like that old saying . . . twenty years from now, we'll regret the things we *didn't* do or say far more than the things we did.

D: Exactly. I felt like an idiot when Sam shot me down—especially the second time. That was brutal. But the greater risk lies in never taking a chance at all—especially when it comes to telling people you care about them.

I mean, what if that person you're afraid of approaching turns out to be your new best friend? What if they feel the same way about you as you do about them? What if they're scared too and hoping you'll make the first move?

What if they end up being "the one"?

Lucky Break

D: Once Sam finally agreed to go on a date with me, I celebrated just like any guy would—by playing a spirited game of flag football.

Every year, our church held a flag football tournament to raise money for missions. As it happened, that year the tournament landed on the same day as our first official date. Could I have skipped the game? Sure. Was I going to? Not in a million years.

Midway through the second quarter, I was playing deep safety, and the other team had the ball. As soon as the ball was snapped, the quarterback began staring down the wide receiver. I made a beeline toward the guy, hoping to intercept it. Unfortunately, the ball was thrown too low for me to make a play. As the receiver reached down to make the catch, I lunged to grab his flags, and he elbowed me right in the nose.

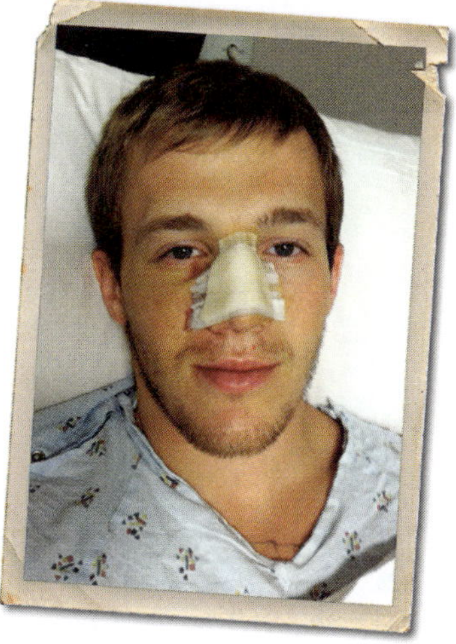

The next thing I knew, there was blood pouring out of my nose, and my eyes were watering so much I could barely even see. As I stumbled blindly toward the sideline, I heard one of my buddies call out, "Hey, Dan, where are you going?"

I turned in the direction of his voice and said, "That guy just broke my nose."

Thinking I was being melodramatic, he clapped back, "No, he didn't."

"Yes," I snapped back, "he did!"

After taking a closer look, he deduced, "Oh, yeah. Dude, that's totally broken." He led me to the first aid area, where the nurse confirmed that my nose was, in fact, broken.

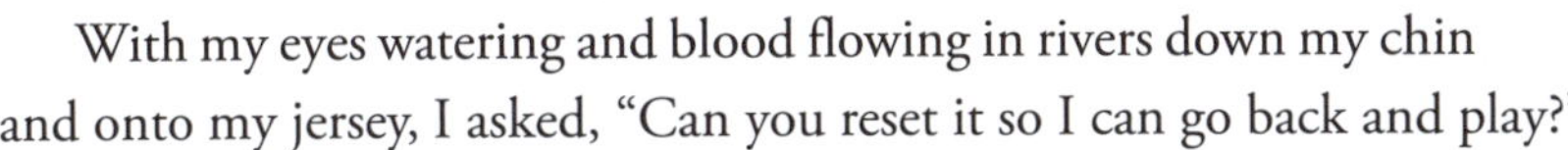

With my eyes watering and blood flowing in rivers down my chin and onto my jersey, I asked, "Can you reset it so I can go back and play?"

She took one look at me. "Are you serious? I can't fix this. You're going to need surgery. Or at the very least an ER visit!"

Now, at this point, most people would have just called it a day and gone to the hospital. Me, I signed a waiver promising not to hold the church liable if I collapsed or bled out, and went right back into the game.

Fortunately for everybody, I ended up being far too bleary-eyed to keep playing, so after staggering around the field for a few minutes, I finally threw in the towel and asked one of my friends to drive me to the hospital. But first I called Sam.

"Hey, babe, it's me. I know we're supposed to go on a date tonight, but I just broke my nose."

S: I'll be the first to admit, I did not see that coming. "Oh my gosh," I said. "What happened? Are you okay?"

D: "I got elbowed in the face playing flag football, but I'll be fine." At this point, both of my eyes were starting to turn black and blue. "I just wanted to let you know I might be a little late."

IF WE INSIST ON WAITING UNTIL EVERYTHING IS JUST RIGHT TO MAKE OUR MOVE, WE RUN THE RISK OF SPENDING OUR ENTIRE LIFE ON HOLD.

S: Was he serious? I mean, the guy had a broken nose, and he was on his way to the hospital. And he was *still* planning to take me out that night? "Are you sure?" I asked. "We could always go out another night."

D: Listen, after waiting for almost a year to take Sam out, they could have amputated my leg that afternoon and I *still* would have gone on that date.

"I'm positive." I was also starting to feel a little lightheaded and nauseous.

S: A few hours later, Dan showed up at my door with two swollen eyes and a very crooked nose, and I all but fell in love with him on the spot. I mean, I could tell just by looking at him that he had to be in an obscene amount of pain, and yet there he was. He'd even left his trademark baseball cap at home and combed his hair!

D: Count your blessings, babe. I don't do that for just anyone.

S: Well, consider them counted, because I felt very valued. We ended up going to one of those Japanese steak houses where they cook your food right on the table in front of you. I love sushi, but not the raw kind. I like the fried shrimp tempura covered in cream cheese and avocado and dipped in Yum Yum sauce—you know, the *good* kind of sushi.

D: Yeah . . . I'm not a fan of either kind. How seaweed, cold rice, and raw shrimp could sound appetizing to anyone, I'll never know. But I wanted to impress Sam, so when she asked if I would like to try her "sushi" roll, I smiled and said, "I'd love to!" Thanks to my broken nose, I couldn't taste or smell anything, but the texture was still too mushy for my liking. So I choked down a bite or two, then insisted that Sam enjoy the rest of the roll.

S: And all this time I thought you were just being polite.

D: Oh, I *was* being polite. Otherwise, I'd have spit that vile slop right out into my napkin. Anyway, Sam ate her weight in fried tempura, and we ended up having a great time.

S: We really did. In fact, I think about that day often.

D: Aw, that's so sweet! Is it because I persevered through pain and did everything I could to make it the best first date ever?

S: Actually, it's because it's the only time I've ever gotten you to try sushi. Come to think of it, we ought to break your nose more often.

Let 'Er Rip!

D: I think the point Sam was *trying* to make was that if I'd postponed our date until my nose was picture-perfect, we would have missed out on what ended up being a spectacular first date doing something Sam loved. Because I can promise you this: had I been able to breathe or actually taste food, there's no way we'd have gone to a sushi joint! Not to mention that I didn't end up getting that corrective surgery for another five years, and that's a heck of a long time to wait!

S: Dan's right. Sometimes you just have to move forward—even if the circumstances aren't ideal. Because let's face it: life rarely lines up perfectly, and if we insist on waiting until everything is just right to make our move, we run the risk of spending our entire life on hold.

I stumbled across a meme once that said, "Don't wait for the perfect moment. Take the moment and make it perfect!" That's exactly what Dan did. The circumstances surrounding our first date might not have been ideal, but that's what made it so special. The fact that he was willing to power through the agony of a freshly broken nose just so we could spend time together meant the world to me. It also taught me more about Dan, his character, and how he genuinely felt about me than a "normal" dinner date ever could have.

D: If all I had planned for that evening was grabbing a burger or going to the movies with the guys, I probably would have stayed home, taken a few aspirin, and gone to bed early. But when something is as important to you as that date with Sam was to me, you don't put it off—even if the timing isn't quite right.

For example, we love going to the beach, and so do our kids. We try to go to Florida several times a year—even if it's a busy time for us professionally or a stretch financially. If we can't get a decent price on plane tickets, we drive. If gas prices are high, we see if we can find another couple to come along and split the cost. If Sam's running behind on her social media commitments, or I have a podcast to record, we bring our laptops with us and take care of these things from the road. Whatever we need to do to make those trips happen, we do it, because it's important to us to get away and spend time together as a family.

S: If we always waited until we had extra money socked away, we'd probably never go, because—let's face it—between car repairs, the kids' schedules, the dog, our health—there's always something that comes up. Plus, when you work in social media, there's always something that needs to be done right away. I can't even remember the last time we both had a free weekend, let alone a free week. Whatever your unique circumstances, we all face things that require our money, time, and attention. This is precisely why we try to be proactive about spending what we have on the things that matter.

It's like that old saying: "On their deathbed, nobody will say, 'I wish I spent more time at the office.'" As much as I love what I do, there is not—nor will there ever be—an Instagram post, a Facebook reel, or a TikTok video that's more important to me than Dan and the kids. We only get about eighteen summers with our kids, and it goes by super fast! That's why I will never regret setting aside my to-do list or scrimping for a few months to spend quality time with our kids. Work and bills will always be there, but we're only going to have seven-year-old Canyon and five-year-old Ember for one year.

D: Speaking of which, I know some people hold off on having kids until they have a specific amount of money in their savings account. Of course, it's helpful to have a little extra money set aside, but the reality is, there will always be something that dips into your savings—the water heater breaks, the car needs new tires, or this year's bonus was less than you expected. But the thing kids need most are things money can't buy: time, attention, and love. We were flat broke when we had Canyon, and even more broke when we had Ember. But we believed it was the right time, and we trusted that God would provide, even if we didn't have it all figured out yet. If we'd waited to start a family until we were in a great place financially, it would *still* be just the two of us. Heck, if we'd waited until we were financially solvent before we got married, there might not even *be* "the two of us."

Are You Ready for This?

D: True story—when I asked Sam's mom for her blessing to get married, she said no—and I mean an emphatic no.

S: It's not that my mom didn't like Dan—they actually got along really well. I think she was just carrying a lot of pain and hurt from her relationship with my dad, and she was worried that the same thing might happen to me. I can't fault her for that.

D: I think she was also afraid of losing you.

S: I'm sure that was part of it. It had been just the three of us for so long, I think she just wasn't ready to let go yet. So she tried to buy a little extra time.

BEING ADVENTUROUS ISN'T ABOUT MAKING RECKLESS OR FLIPPANT DECISIONS. IT'S ABOUT BEING WILLING TO TAKE CALCULATED RISKS AND NOT LETTING FEAR STAND IN THE WAY OF TRYING NEW THINGS.

D: In the most Robin way possible . . .

I had barely walked in the front door when Sam's mom sighed, sat down on the couch, and said, "I already know what this is about, so you might as well just go ahead."

I said, "Okay. Well, the thing is, I really love your daughter. We've been together for a long time now, and I would very much like to marry her."

"So are you *telling* me you're marrying her," she asked. "Or are you asking for my permission?"

I paused for a second. "I'm . . . asking for your blessing."

She stared at me, emotionless, then said, "Well, you do *not* have my blessing."

Wow, I thought, *tough room.* "Can I ask why?"

"Because I don't think you're ready."

"What do you mean?"

"Do you have health insurance?"

"No."

"Dental?"

"No."

"Vision?"

"No."

"Life insurance?"

"No."

"Do you have a 401(k)?"

"No."

For the record, this was not at all how I had imagined this conversation going.

"Well, Dan, what if something happens to one of you?" she asked. "How are you planning to pay for it? Samantha is waiting tables, and you work in a warehouse.

Between the two of you, you barely make enough money to cover rent, let alone buy a house. And God forbid something were to happen!"

In fairness, she was right. Neither of us had "careers," and no, we didn't have insurance or a little nest egg to fall back on. But in our minds, we were totally ready. For one thing, we had been together for three years. We'd gone through job changes together and supported each other through hospital visits and major surgeries. We had seen each other at our best and at our worst—happy, sad, angry, sick, with and without makeup, and with and without baseball caps. We had worked through disagreements and stood by each other during the loss of family members. And even though we were very different people, we had a lot in common. We both loved the outdoors, we loved being active, and we were both driven to succeed. Most importantly, we both loved the Lord and were equally committed to putting him first in our relationship and in everything we did. We had even taken a class for engaged couples at our church and spent a great deal of time talking with our pastor and a married couple we respected about commitment and the challenges of being newlyweds.

In one meeting, the couple we were meeting with said, "You will never feel financially ready for marriage or for having kids, but you can't let that keep you from making a choice."

So while I may not have had the perfect job or a nice house with a yard, I did have unconditional love for Sam and a desire to start a future with her. But before I could explain any of this to Robin, she cocked her head to the side and said, "Let me ask you this. If you *were* going to ask her, when were you planning to do it?"

"Sam and I are going to Florida with a bunch of friends next month," I said. "I was planning to ask her there." A look of absolute panic washed over her face.

"Dan," she said, grabbing my arm. "I need you to promise me you won't ask her to marry you."

I thought, *She's kidding, right?* "Sorry, Robin, but I can't promise you that. I *can* promise you that I will pray about it, though." The mood was pretty much shot at that point, so we opted to skip dinner and call it a night.

S: As soon as Dan walked out of my mom's house, she called me. "Just so you know, Samantha, he's planning to propose to you while you're in Florida next month."

For the record, I knew Dan was thinking about proposing. I mean, we'd had conversations about it. But, dang, talk about spilling the beans!

Then she said, "You have to promise me that if he asks you, you'll say no."

I loved my mom, and I knew that deep down, she had my best interests at heart. But I also loved Dan, so there was no way I was going to make that promise.

"Mom, I can't do that," I said. "We've both been praying about this for a while now, and we feel like we're ready."

"I'm not saying you can *never* get married," she backpedaled. "I just want him to hold a steady job for two years and set aside some money for a house and emergencies. I want you to have some security."

Security was incredibly important to my mom, and I get it. After all, she had to raise two daughters on her own, so she knew how hard—and expensive—life can be. But to expect us to put our lives on hold for two years or until we had a certain dollar amount set aside felt so arbitrary—and frankly, a little ridiculous.

D: Robin had a point about wanting me to have insurance and a steady job, but *my* first two priorities were my relationship with God and my commitment to Sam. I could have every type of "worldly" insurance available, but to me, my relationship with the Lord is the best insurance there is. And if my commitment to Sam wasn't rock solid, who's to say I would stick around when things got tough? Robin could talk about dental plans and 401(k)s all day long, but in my mind, I had all the insurance I needed. So whether she approved or not, unless I received a strong urging from the Lord to do otherwise, I had every intention of asking Sam to be my wife.

Some Monsters Aren't Real

D & S: Please hear us out: we're not saying that even if your parents disapprove, you should go ahead and get married anyway, or if your friends have some hesitations about your plan to camp solo in Alaska in December, you should ignore their advice. A great deal of thought, prayer, discussion, and discernment went into our decision, as it should yours, regardless of what decision you're making. Remember, being adventurous isn't about making reckless or flippant decisions. It's about being

THE THING ABOUT FEAR IS THAT A LOT OF IT IS IN OUR HEADS. AND IF WE AREN'T CAREFUL, SOMETHING THAT EXISTS ONLY IN OUR IMAGINATIONS CAN PREVENT US FROM DOING REAL THINGS.

willing to take calculated risks and not letting fear stand in the way of trying new things.

We knew going in that between her personal history and her overly cautious temperament, Robin was going to be a tough sell. That's why she wasn't the only person we talked to. Of course, we valued her opinion—as someone who had gone through a difficult divorce, she offered a valuable perspective. But we also wanted to hear from other people too—people who could balance her pragmatic concerns with encouragement and a positive experience with marriage. That's why we talked at length with our pastor and sought out the mentorship of a couple who had been married for more than thirty years. We wanted to make sure that we were ready and that we knew what we were getting into—the good and the challenging—before we jumped in with both feet.

Did we still have doubts? Heck, yeah. But the more we talked with different people, asked questions, heard their stories, and got a clearer picture of what healthy (and unhealthy) marriages looked like, the more confident we felt.

That's the thing about fear. A lot of it is in our heads. And if we aren't careful, something that exists only in our imaginations can prevent us from doing real things. Like Franklin D. Roosevelt said, "The only thing we have to fear is fear itself." Once you face down that fear, you can do practically anything.

D: When Canyon was really little, he was utterly convinced there was a monster living in his closet—even though he'd never seen or heard it. So one night before bed, I suggested we take a look together while all the lights were on and I was there with him. We walked over to his closet and opened the door. I started rooting through his clothes, asking, "Where is he? Do you see him, buddy? Where's that monster hiding?" Soon, he was crouched down on the floor, pushing all of his shoes and toys out of the way. After a couple of seconds, he stood up and said, "Huh, I guess he's

not in there." And he was fine from that moment on. He just had to face his fear and see for himself that the fear was all in his head.

I used to have a fear of snakes. I have no idea why—I'd never been bitten by one before. Then one day, I went to a pet store and asked if I could hold one. The guy who ran the place set a baby ball python in my hand. Now, I fully expected this thing to slither up my arm and crawl down my shirt, attach itself to my face, or wrap itself around my neck until I stopped breathing. So I just stared at it, waiting—and terrified. But it just sat there, curled up in a little ball. I'm not even sure it was awake. I ended up buying the little guy. In time, it grew to more than four feet long. It used to rest on my shoulders while I studied or watched TV. Just like Canyon and the closet monster, the worst-case sudden-strangulation scenario existed only in my mind, and once I faced my fear, I got over it.

S: It's perfectly normal to be frightened. Fear isn't *all* bad—it can keep us from doing inherently dangerous, downright stupid things, like approaching a wild animal or running outside during a lightning storm. But if we're not careful, it can also keep us from experiencing some truly great things, like seeing a new part of the world, meeting a new friend, getting married, buying a home, taking a new job, starting a family, or going on any number of adventures.

The key is to not let fear—yours or anyone else's—rule your life or make your decisions for you. The goal is to maintain a healthy balance of caution and optimism—to step out in faith and try new things but also seek good counsel and act wisely.

D: One of my favorite verses is 2 Timothy 1:7: "God has not given us a spirit of fear and timidity, but of power, love, and self-discipline." I love that.

God doesn't want us to be afraid. He wants us to go into the world and face our fears and do hard things. But he doesn't want us to be irresponsible or to make rash, ill-informed decisions either. He wants us to lean on each other for support and to advise and encourage each other. Most importantly, he wants us to look to *him* for guidance. That's why Isaiah refers to him as "Wonderful Counselor" (Isaiah 9:6).

At the end of the day, though, the decision is yours.

When You're Feeling Stuck

D & S: While doing your research and seeking the counsel of others before making a major life decision can be incredibly helpful, it's possible to become so overwhelmed with information that you completely freeze up. Psychologists call it analysis paralysis, and we can tell you, the struggle is real.

S: I struggle with this a lot more than Dan does. He's pretty good at making a decision and moving forward. I, on the other hand, tend to get lost in a sea of options and wind up creating an endless stream of pro and con lists in my head. For example, a few years ago, we needed to find an apartment. Dan's only criteria was that it have four walls, a floor, and a ceiling. But then, he's perfectly content to sleep on the wet ground in the woods. Me? I got caught up in a death spiral of considerations: *Which side of town do we want to live on? What school will the kids go to? This place is closer to church, but that one is closer to our friends. I like the kitchen and the floor plan of the two-bedroom better, but if we got the three-bedroom, the kids could each have their own room. I like the corner unit, but the one next to the stairs gets more light. This complex has covered parking, but the apartment is on the third floor and there's no elevator, so it'll be a pain lugging the kids and groceries up and down. Still, it does have central air. Of course, the other place comes with free Wi-Fi, but oh my word, did you see the bathroom?* The more time I have to think about something, the more stuck I get.

D: It's brutal.

S: Tell me about it.

FEAR ISN'T *ALL* BAD. BUT IF WE'RE NOT CAREFUL, IT CAN KEEP US FROM EXPERIENCING SOME TRULY GREAT THINGS.

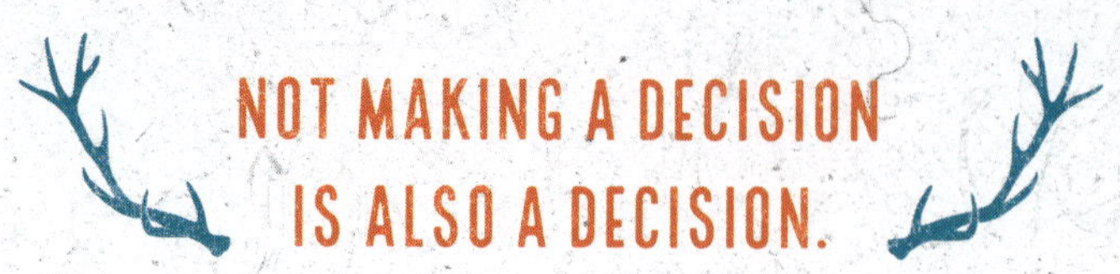

D: No, I'm serious. You should have seen Sam trying to choose an Internet provider. I still wake up screaming.

S: You and me both.

Actually, that reminds me, there's an awesome episode of *The Big Bang Theory* where Sheldon is trying to decide between an Xbox One or a PS4 gaming system, and he is so terrified of making the wrong decision that he does months' worth of research, talks to everyone he knows, and conducts an informal survey, but for each thing he likes about one system, there is something different he likes about the other—one has a better camera, but the other has a removable hard drive; one is smaller and cooler looking, but the larger size of the other system may keep it from overheating; one has more RAM, but the other has some special buffer thing. The episode ends with him sitting on the floor of the electronics store staring at both systems—literally in tears—with his exhausted girlfriend, Amy, begging him to "just pick one!" And that's when it happens. He looks her right in the eye and says, "But what if I'm wrong?"

D: And *that's* the problem. Because let's face it—more often than not, there is no intrinsically right or wrong decision. Whether you paint a room beige or gray, get pepperoni or sausage on your pizza, sign up with Verizon or AT&T, or name your dog Buddy or Spark, your life is not going to be dramatically impacted one way or the other. Yet we convince ourselves that if we make the wrong choice—whatever that may be—it will haunt us until our dying day. And like Sheldon, we freeze and become incapable of making a decision at all.

But here's the thing: not making a decision? That's also a decision. But it's a decision that you're letting fear and uncertainty make for you.

Now, do some decisions turn out badly? Oh, yeah. We hated our first apartment. But guess what? We didn't have to stay there forever. Very few decisions are irreversible. People move. They change jobs. They reinvest in a different stock. They trade in one car for another. They repaint. They return the shoes they bought online, and they vow to never use self-tanner again.

We've made a ton of purchases that we ended up regretting. We've also made a lot of bad business decisions—but we're still here. And we're smarter and stronger for the experience.

Making bad decisions is part of life. It's how you learn. It's how you grow. The only way you stop learning and growing is if you don't do anything.

It should be acknowledged here that some decisions are weightier than others. The person you choose to marry involves making a lifelong commitment. The decision to add a child to your family requires love and sacrifice for the rest of your life. These aren't decisions to be made lightly, but God has given us minds and hearts to ask good questions and to make wise choices, and he promises to guide us along the way.

So do your research, ask questions, talk to people you trust, and pray about it. But at some point, if you want to fully experience life, you've gotta jump in and go for it!

. . . And We Did!

D: Sam's mom may have spilled the beans on my plan to propose in Florida, but I still wanted to make the moment special. So in the weeks leading up to our trip, I got all our friends to film a video montage where they talked about how much they loved Sam and how excited they were about our relationship.

One evening, I took Sam for a walk along the beach, while, unbeknownst to her, our friends were setting up candles along the private dock that stretched out into the bay. By the time we made our way back to the dock, our friends had vanished, and it was just me, Sam, and the engagement ring I had hidden in my pocket.

I walked her to the end of the dock, where our friends had set up a folding chair, a laptop, and a small bowl filled with water.

S: Dan asked me to sit down, then he hit play, and as the screen filled with images of our friends telling us how happy they were for us and how much they loved our relationship, Dan sat on the dock and gently washed the sand off of my feet. It was absolutely beautiful. As soon as the video ended, he got on one knee and nervously

stumbled through a speech that I kinda got the impression he had tried to memorize but forgot once the moment actually hit.

D: It did sound a lot better in my head.

S: It didn't matter. I was so moved by the video, the foot washing, and how much you genuinely cared about me, I barely heard a word you said.

D: All I know is that when I finally popped the question, Sam took my hand, smiled at me, and with tears in her eyes, said the words I'd been dreaming about since she served me that first cookie monster protein shake: "Not until you get a steady job and some life insurance."

S: And also . . . "Yes."

D: Was everything perfect? Not by a long shot. In addition to screwing up my big speech, I also had a miserable sunburn and was in excruciating pain the entire time. And of course, we didn't have Robin's blessing. But there was no way I was going to let any of that keep me from asking Sam the question I'd waited years to ask.

S: The first thing the next morning, I texted my mom:

> Hey Mom, just want to let you know that Dan proposed last night and I said yes. We're going on a boat ride today, so I'm turning my phone off, but I'll talk to you later. I love you.

D: Robin did eventually come around, thanks in no small part to our pastor, who assured her that Sam and I had, in fact, taken all the proper precautionary steps, had completed our premarital counseling, and were very much ready to start our lives together. I also apologized for anything I might have said or done to cause her concern and promised I would work hard to earn her trust.

S: It also helped her, I think, to see how wonderfully Dan and I got along, and how caring and supportive he was throughout our engagement. For most of our relationship, she just thought of him as this goofy college kid who had a crush on her daughter. But by the time the big day rolled around, she had started to see him the way I did—as an incredibly kind, respectful, loving, and hysterically funny man (with a killer six-pack) who was willing to do whatever he needed to do to take care of me—including getting some insurance.

D: We might not have had our careers all mapped out, a hundred grand in the bank, or a 401(k) collecting interest for our retirement, but we loved each other unconditionally and we shared a strong faith in God and a commitment not just to do life together but to *enjoy* life together, no matter what came our way. We even worked it into our vows:

I take you to be my best friend, my faithful partner, and my one true love. I promise to encourage you, inspire you, and love you truly through good times and bad. I will forever be there to laugh with you, to lift you up when you're down, and to love you unconditionally through all our adventures in life together.

It might not have been the traditional "I take you to be my lawfully wedded" script, but every word had meaning to us, and that was all the insurance we needed.

IF YOU WAIT UNTIL

Everything Is Perfect

BEFORE MOVING FORWARD,

YOU'RE GOING TO

MISS OUT ON AN AWFUL LOT.

SOMETIMES YOU JUST HAVE TO

Dive In

BEFORE EVERYTHING IS

COMPLETELY LINED UP.

3

JUST WHEN YOU THOUGHT *Your Life Was Over*

S: "Babe, is everything okay in there?" Dan asked me.

"Yep! Almost done!" I knew he was anxious to hit the road. I just needed a few more minutes—three, to be exact. At least that's what the package said.

It was a big day. We were picking up our new puppy from the breeder. Well, technically, *we* were the breeder. It's a long story.

Actually, you know what? We've got three minutes . . .

Dan had always wanted a hunting dog, and shortly before our second wedding anniversary, we got one! Well, we *thought* we did. We spent several nights on Craigslist looking for a Lab with a good bloodline, preferably one that was already trained for hunting. We came across several, but one in particular stood out to us. He was an adorable chocolate Lab, AKC registered, *and* within our price range. We fell in love with him instantly—or I did, anyway.

The second I saw him, I started envisioning our life with him, so we messaged the owner. But in true Craigslist fashion, it turned out he was already spoken for. I was so upset, I couldn't bring myself to even look at another dog, but Dan spent a few more days searching. Just when I thought all hope was lost, Dan found Rudy—a seven-year-old "retired" AKC-registered black Lab.

"Didn't we want a puppy, though?" I asked Dan.

"Yeah," he said, "but this one's already trained, and the guy isn't even asking anything for him—just a good home."

"Okay, might as well take a look." I have to admit, I was a little disappointed, but he was mostly going to be Dan's dog anyway, and free AKC-registered Labs don't come along every day. We messaged Rudy's owner, who promptly invited us to meet him.

D: Since Sam's enthusiasm had waned a bit after losing out on the puppy, I drove the hour and a half to meet Rudy by myself. When I showed up, I discovered a mildly overweight but extremely energetic dog. The owner walked me through the different commands Rudy knew and threw a rubber training toy to show me how well he could retrieve. There was no question that he was a great retriever, but I couldn't help but notice that Rudy showed zero interest in me. Still, I decided to roll the dice, and I'm glad I did, because by the time we got home, Rudy was 100 percent my dog.

From the moment I brought him home, no matter who we were around or who we introduced him to, his focus was completely on me and nothing else. Even when friends or family tried to play fetch with him, he'd get the ball and bring it right back to me.

S: I have to admit, it was a little frustrating that Rudy didn't show any interest in me, but he absolutely adored Dan, and that's all that mattered. The two of them were inseparable. Then one day, Dan took him to meet with a professional trainer.

D: The guy took one look at him and said, "I hate to tell you this, Dan, but you've basically got yourself a glorified fetcher. He'll bring things back to you, but he's not going to scare up any game. He's got a good bloodline, though. You might want to consider breeding him."

S: We spent the next several weeks driving Rudy down to Ozark for a series of "playdates" with another AKC-registered hunting Lab named Britti. Fortunately, Rudy and Britti got along famously, and a few months later, Britti's owner called to let us know that Rudy was officially a daddy. And as the unofficial in-laws, Dan and I got our pick of the litter, free of charge.

The following weekend, we drove down to see the puppies and—with no idea what the indicators of a great hunter would be at this stage—picked out a cute little male, who, for all we knew, could either grow up to be the greatest hunting dog in the world or end up being an unholy terror that would eat our sofa, tear the doors off our kitchen cabinets, and poop on the dryer. Either way, we finally had our little Gunner.

For the next six weeks, Dan waited impatiently for Gunner to be fully weaned so he could go get him and bring him home.

In the meantime, we'd had a few "playdates" of our own, and now . . .

"Babe," Dan called out from the bedroom. "What's going on in there?"

I just stood there staring at two pale pink lines. I glanced down at my phone. It hadn't even been three minutes yet.

While I waited for the test to fully register, I did some quick arithmetic. We hadn't necessarily been trying to get pregnant. Then again, we hadn't *not* been trying either. Let's put it this way: we hadn't been anywhere near as calculated about it as we were with the puppy.

I don't even know what made me decide to check that morning. Aside from a few headaches, I hadn't really experienced any symptoms. Though I *had* recently downed an entire jar of Vlasic Kosher Dills in one sitting, which, in retrospect, was probably a sign.

D: When Sam came out of the bathroom, she had a smile on her face a mile wide. The second I saw her, I knew. Of course, the pregnancy test she was holding was also a bit of a tip-off. "Are you . . . ? Are we . . . ? Is that . . . ?" I stammered, pointing at the little white stick in her hand.

"Yup," she said, beaming. "I'm pregnant."

I was so caught off guard, I didn't even know what to say. I just pulled her into a giant bear hug, kissed the top of her head, and softly whispered into her ear, "I love you so much. Now let's go get our dog."

S: Okay, so not exactly a Hallmark card, but in fairness, we were both in shock—excited and thrilled beyond reason—but definitely in shock. In fact, the full reality of it didn't settle in until later that night, when we found ourselves getting up every two hours to sit with a whimpering puppy. Dan smiled at me, bleary-eyed, and said, "I guess this is our life now."

Shock and exhaustion aside, we couldn't have been happier about the prospect of becoming parents. Our friends, however, had a slightly different perspective.

Things Will Never Be the Same (They'll Be Even Better)

D & S: We were the first ones in our friend group to get pregnant. And since we also tended to be the first ones in our friend group to say things like, "Hey, let's all go camping [or hiking or climbing or hunting] this weekend," our little announcement got a slightly different reaction than we were expecting.

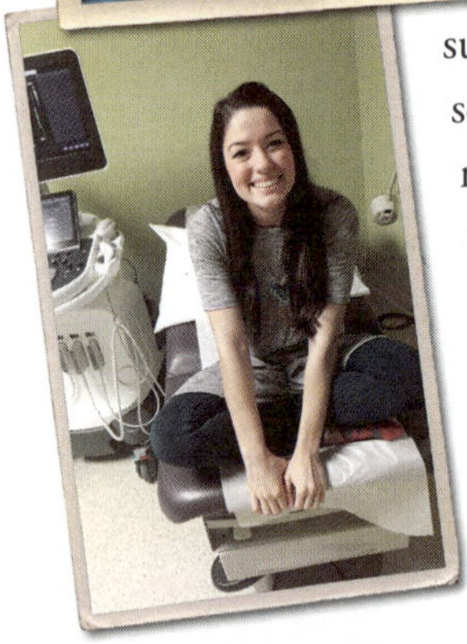

Virtually every "Aw, congratulations!" was immediately followed by some variation of, "Well, I guess that's the end of the road for you two," "Guess we just lost a hunting buddy," or "Say goodbye to all your upcoming road trips."

In our minds, the adventure was just beginning! In theirs, our lives had essentially ended the second the line turned pink.

D: To be fair, I got where they were coming from. I have three older sisters, all of whom had kids before Sam and I did, and I could see how much their lives changed when they became parents. All of a sudden, they had to think about things like the kids' bedtime, school schedules, and sports practices. I understood that babies and kids aren't mini adults, and there are inevitable shifts when you're responsible for a small human who is dependent on you. Still, we'd seen some people who put their entire lives on hold as soon as they became parents, and that's not what we wanted. That's why we promised each other early in our relationship that if we had kids, instead of restructuring our entire lives around them, we would simply incorporate our kids into whatever we were already doing.

S: This started before our kids were even born. When I was pregnant with Canyon, Dan and I kept working out together, hiking, camping, and traveling with our friends all the way through my eighth month. I even auditioned for a dance team at church two weeks before my due date. The day I was discharged from the hospital, we went to a bonfire with a bunch of our friends—and we brought Canyon with us.

D: Generally speaking, newborns spend the majority of their first few weeks sleeping, so he had no objections. We didn't change our plans because of Canyon; we simply incorporated Canyon into our plans.

S: As for the dance team I auditioned for, our first practice was the week after Canyon was born, so I just tucked him into his stroller and rolled him right in. I'm telling you, that kid was a hit! All the women on the team just loved him. In fact, he got doted on and fussed over at those dance rehearsals more than he ever would have at home. It took me a couple of weeks to get my groove back post-pregnancy, but it felt great to be out doing something I really enjoyed with my son—even if he did sleep through most of it.

D: Seriously, that kid slept like a champ. Two months later, we took him along on a climbing trip with some friends, and he spent the entire morning sleeping in a little hammock we hung at the base of the rock face. It was perfect, because the trees provided plenty of shade, and even if he got fidgety, the high walls of the hammock kept him safe and snug. (And yes, we do recognize the position we found ourselves in is not possible for every baby!)

S: Canyon was never once left unattended. We took turns climbing the rock face and rappelling down, and whoever was at the bottom kept an eye on him. He was going to spend the entire morning sleeping anyway—we just instituted a slight change in location.

D: A few months later, when we were living in Colorado (another long story—we'll get to that in a bit), a bunch of our friends from Missouri came out to visit. One afternoon, they decided to climb Longs Peak. They just assumed that Sam and I wouldn't be able to go, so when we started gathering our stuff, they said, "What about Canyon? Who's going to watch him while you're gone?"

S: Dan just laughed. "We are. He's coming with us." They were skeptical at first, but we bundled him up in a baby carrier and took turns hiking with him.

D: Instead of thinking of our baby as an anchor, weighing us down and keeping us moored in one place, we thought of him as an awesome new hiking and camping accessory that made our adventures that much more fun and memorable. By the time he was nine months old, Canyon had been on multiple hikes and rock-climbing expeditions and had attended countless bonfires, cookouts, and picnics. After a while, our friends started thinking of him as one of the gang.

S: We still had a schedule for him. We just weren't super strict about it to the point that we would cancel our plans. And because he went along to so many different places, he got used to riding in the car, sleeping in various environments, and being around a lot of people. Fortunately, Canyon was super chill and could sleep pretty much anywhere—in part, because Dan made a point of exposing him to a lot of background noise from the get-go.

THERE'S NO ONE-SIZE-FITS-ALL APPROACH WHEN IT COMES TO PARENTING.

D: It was a given that any kid of mine would have to deal with a fair amount of noise and chaos—especially in the morning. I do a lot of hunting, so it's not unusual for me to be up crashing around the house at 3 a.m., and I didn't want Sam to have to calm a crying baby every time I went out. So for the first few weeks of his life, I made a point of making a lot of noise so he would get used to sleeping through it. Right after we got home from the hospital, I built and installed a set of shelves and hung a flat-screen TV in the living room while he slept less than ten feet away in his bassinet.

We weren't blasting with dynamite or running an air compressor—we knew better than to expose him to anything louder than 70 decibels (and for the record, most vacuums are between 70 and 80, and even a blender is 85)—but I had power tools going, Sam was vacuuming up the dust as I went, and we were both talking to each other over the noise. And while Canyon was a little fidgety at first, he eventually hunkered down and slept right through it.

S: Actually, a lot of pediatricians recommend getting your kids used to a certain amount of noise early on. Otherwise, you wind up tiptoeing around them, and that's when they've got you! All of a sudden, you're modifying everything to accommodate their sleeping schedule. Getting Canyon used to a certain amount of noise and activity early on allowed us to continue doing a lot of the things that Dan and I loved—only now, we were doing them together as a family.

One morning when Canyon was about six months old, I was still in bed when I heard a gunshot in the field right behind us. A few seconds later, Dan called to tell me he'd shot a deer. I wanted to see it, so I woke Canyon up, put on his little camo sweater, and took him to the field so we could see Daddy's deer together. Later that night, Dan had to process the meat, which is a two-person job and—trust me on this—best done outside, so there we were at 10 p.m. with little headlamps on, processing a deer while Canyon slept in his bassinet next to us.

As he got a little older, we took him four-wheeling and camping—Dan even bought him a little cork gun and took him out "duck hunting" with him. These are all things we genuinely enjoy doing, and because we introduced Canyon to them when he was young, he now enjoys doing them too.

D: We know what you're thinking: sure, you could do that with *your* kid, but not mine. Believe me, we know we hit the proverbial jackpot with Canyon. He was super adaptable and rarely fussed, regardless of what was going on around him. Our daughter, Ember, however, was a different story. That kid could hear a pin drop and be on the edge of her bed crying hysterically for hours.

S: When Ember was around a year old, we drove up to Estes Park for the day while Dan's parents were visiting. Well, Ember wasn't a huge fan of the car, and she cried the entire ride there. At any point, we could have canceled the trip, turned around, and gone back home, but what would that have accomplished? We knew she'd eventually wear herself out, and Canyon didn't care. In fact, he was out like a light one car seat over. So we just pushed through.

D: Of course, if Ember (or Canyon) had been sick, we would have canceled. We just weren't going to let a fussy one-year-old call the shots for everyone else. For one thing, rewarding a tantrum would have established a bad precedent. The choice was hers: she could either cry herself to sleep or chill out and enjoy the ride, but either way, we were going to Estes Park. Turning around and ruining the trip for everyone wasn't an option.

Kids are a lot more resilient than people give them credit for. Once we got there, Ember was fine. The weather was beautiful, we had a great day, and by the time we left, she was so exhausted from being out in the fresh air that she slept the whole way home.

S: We're not saying it's easy. We get that every kid is different and some kids require special accommodations and a gentler touch. There's no one-size-fits-all approach when it comes to parenting, and everyone has to figure out what works best for their family.

D: We just encourage you not to automatically assume that having kids means you can no longer do the things that bring you joy and make you who you are. Generally speaking, most experts agree that the best thing we can do for our kids is to maintain a happy, healthy marriage. For our relationship, that means going on adventures together and doing the things that make us *us*.

That's why when Canyon was only a few weeks old, we started leaving him with Sam's mom once a week so we could have a date night. As of this writing, our kids are seven and five, and Sam's mom still takes them every Friday so we can have a night to just be "Dan and Sam" as opposed to "Dad and Mom."

S: Spending time with your kids is important, but when you do it at the expense of having quality time together as a couple, it's easy to grow apart. If you focus on your relationship first and make a conscious effort to bring your kids into activities that you and your spouse already enjoy, you can all grow closer together.

TIPS FOR TRAVELING WITH KIDS {AKA HOW TO KEEP KIDS ENTERTAINED BEYOND SCREENS}

- Pack lots of snacks! Create your own "snacklebox" (snack + tacklebox).
- Have flexibility and patience. Things will go wrong, so do your best to go with the flow.
- Prepare games to pass the time (for example, license plate bingo, the alphabet game, I spy, Would You Rather?, twenty questions, name that tune).
- Bring little surprise gifts for longer trips.

D: We should also note here that parenting is more than a two-person job. It's critical to have people in your life who love your kids and give you a break, especially during those early years when your kids need so much from you. We've been grateful to have extended family who love our kids and take them for the evening

IF YOU BRING YOUR KIDS INTO ACTIVITIES THAT YOU AND YOUR SPOUSE ALREADY ENJOY, YOU CAN ALL GROW CLOSER TOGETHER.

or the weekend—or sometimes an entire week. When Ember was young and we lived in Colorado, with no family close by, we would trade off date nights with our friends. Once a month we would watch their son while they went on a date, and once a month they watched our kids while we went on a date. It was a huge blessing in that season. It's worth the effort to find people you trust who will invest in your kids—and in your relationship too.

S: Again, it doesn't have to be anything elaborate or expensive. The whole point is just to enjoy spending time together as a family. Maybe for you that means going to a restaurant once a week, having a family movie night, hitting the bike trail together, or buying tickets to see your favorite sports team. For us, it means doing things together outside and hitting the open road.

What Hassle?

D & S: One of our favorite things to do as a family is going to the beach. And because we thought Canyon and Ember might enjoy playing with kids their age there, one year we invited our friends on a road trip to Florida. "What do you say—all eight of us in one car for a quick fourteen-hour drive?"

You should have seen the look of shock on their faces. "That sounds chaotic! Besides, will we even have time to relax and enjoy it with kids running around?"

We get it. Traveling with kids can be "eight people in one vehicle" type of chaos, but for us, the trade-off was worth it. We got to spend time with our friends and our kids, and if spending an afternoon helping them build a sandcastle or collect seashells meant we got a little less time to lie out in the sun or read a book, then so be it. After all, what's the point of going on a family vacation if you're not going to spend time together as a family?

D: Is traveling with kids more involved than traveling by yourself or with another adult? Of course, it is. Still, that's no reason to deprive yourself of a trip you'd love to take. In fact, having the kids along just makes the experience that much more memorable! Take it from a couple who spent the better part of a year traveling all over the country with two kids under eight in an RV. Seriously, it's not as complicated as you might think.

S: Everyone thinks, *Oh, man, we're gonna have to drag a thousand toys along with us*, but you really don't. Obviously, you need the essentials—clothes, diapers, a few favorite snacks—but you'd be surprised how easily kids can amuse themselves with something as simple as an empty box, a stick they found along a hiking trail, or a bag of seashells they picked up on the beach. When Ember was about nine months old, I took her with me on a flight from Denver to St. Louis, and she kept herself amused for half an hour just stuffing Cheerios into an empty water bottle.

D: Besides, when you're on vacation, the change of scenery alone is usually enough to keep them occupied. Our kids have spent hours on camping trips playing with rocks, tree branches, pine cones, and even piles of dirt! When we go to the beach, we just bring along a couple of plastic pails and shovels—the sand, the water, and the miles of seaweed, seashells, and sand dollars take care of the rest. The whole point of getting away is to leave your normal life behind and experience something different. The more "home" you bring with you, the less of an adventure it is for the kids—and for you!

S: The key is to be patient and play the long game. Don't expect everything to go perfectly the first—or

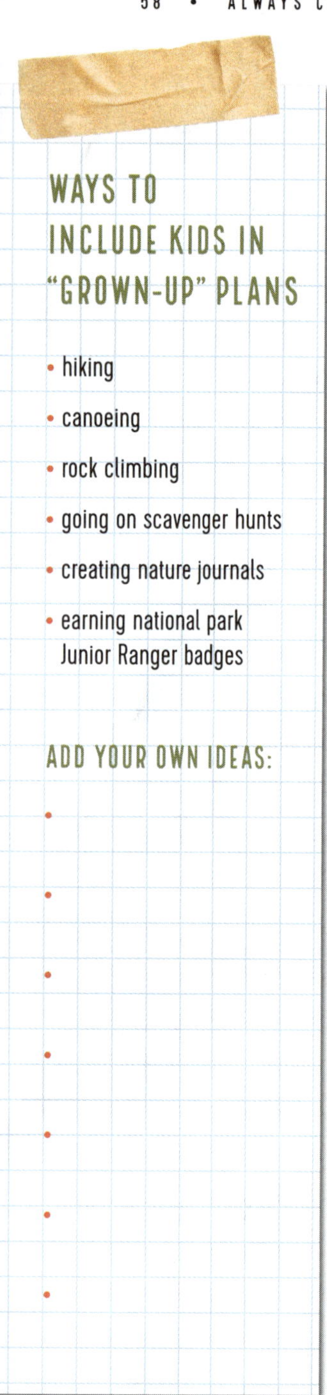

WAYS TO INCLUDE KIDS IN "GROWN-UP" PLANS

- hiking
- canoeing
- rock climbing
- going on scavenger hunts
- creating nature journals
- earning national park Junior Ranger badges

ADD YOUR OWN IDEAS:

-
-
-
-
-
-
-

even the second—time. Don't jump ship or give up too soon! It might take a couple of days for your kids to adjust to a new routine and discover that they can, in fact, make it through a day without their video games or iPads. But if you stick with it, in time, life on the road will become like second nature to them.

Canyon and Ember love going places with us. And more often than not, there are no toys or electronics involved—it's just the four of us and a trail, a tent, or a beach blanket. In fact, as soon as we get back from one adventure, they usually start asking, "When's our next road trip?" Now that they've gotten a taste of it, they're hungry for it! And your kids will be too—you just have to give them a chance.

Kids Will Be Kids

D & S: It goes without saying that kids will be kids. They're gonna get tired, hot, and hangry. At some point, they'll spill something in the car, fight over who gets to sit next to "the good window," throw someone's shoe out of said window, lose something, break something, or leave something behind in a gas station bathroom. And you know what? You just have to roll with it.

D: When Ember was a baby, we went camping in the mountains with my cousin Wayne, his wife, Tiffany, and their three kids, who ranged in age from two to six. One night, after setting up the tents and getting everything unpacked, Sam, Wayne, Tiffany, and I were sitting around the fire relaxing while the kids were all scattered around the campsite playing.

All of a sudden, I heard something hit our Denali. Sam was busy taking care of Ember, so I got up and walked to the front of the vehicle. There was Canyon, with a handful of rocks, drawing circles on the side of the vehicle—with said rocks! I

kid you not, there were dozens of little circles carved into the paint, all along the side of the truck.

Now, this particular truck was Sam's pride and joy, so I thought, *Oh, my goodness! Sam's gonna freak when she sees this!* As if on cue, Sam called out, "What happened? Did he break something?"

"Trust me," I called back, "you don't wanna see it." So naturally, she came right over. Her jaw dropped, and she said, "Oh, you have *got* to be kidding me!"

Honestly, it was hard to know whether to laugh or cry. On the one hand, the kid had totally destroyed the paint job. Even if we could buff out some of the milder scratches, we were still looking at hundreds of dollars' worth of damage. And yet how could we get mad at him? He didn't do it on purpose. Well, actually, he did. But he didn't *know* he was doing anything wrong. Canyon loved drawing, so to him, the truck was a blank canvas and, as fate would have it, a pile of rocks became his medium.

For the record, we chose option C: we cried internally, kicked ourselves for letting a two-year-old out of our sight for fifteen minutes, then knelt down and gently said, "Hey, buddy, please don't draw on the truck, okay? If you want to draw, use your finger or a stick and draw in the dirt." And he did.

Now, some people might say, "See? That's why you don't travel with little kids!" But in fairness, this could just as easily have happened at home in our own driveway. No matter where they are, kids are going to do kid things. At the end of the day, you have to ask yourself, *What's more important to me—my kids or my stuff?*

It's Not about You

D & S: The bottom line is that parenting is an inherently selfless act. You're constantly making sacrifices. When your kids are little, you give up sleep; when they get a little bigger, you give up quiet time; when they learn how to grab hold of things,

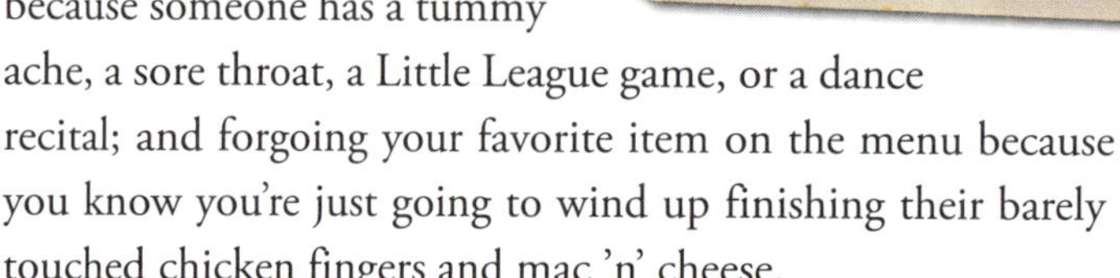

you can kiss a lot of your prized possessions goodbye. You find yourself watching *Bluey* instead of the game on Saturday; missing out on a hunting trip you've been looking forward to because someone has a tummy ache, a sore throat, a Little League game, or a dance recital; and forgoing your favorite item on the menu because you know you're just going to wind up finishing their barely touched chicken fingers and mac 'n' cheese.

From the moment your kids are born, what you want takes a back seat to what they need. But what they need more than anything is you—you spending time with them, teaching them, and introducing them to the world around them. Once you discover how much fun it is to do things together, this becomes what you want as well.

D: So much of our enjoyment comes from watching our kids learn and have fun. When Canyon was little, he loved "helping" me build things. I didn't want him to get hurt, so all I did was let him help pull the trigger on the drill, but he loved it! Yeah, it slowed me down, but watching his face light up when that drill powered a screw into the wood was worth every extra minute that project took.

S: When Ember was little, she loved helping me bake cookies. She'd pour bags of chocolate chips into the batter and help me decorate cakes and cookies. Some of them turned out a little wonky, and a lot of ingredients ended up on the floor, but I will always cherish the memories of her little frosting-covered face.

D: As they've gotten older, we've started taking the kids to places we loved going when we were dating and newly married. Even though we've been to some of these places dozens of times, when we go back with Canyon and Ember, it's like seeing it all for the first time because now we're seeing it through their eyes.

The thing is, we don't just love our kids; we *like* our kids too. That's why we take them with us almost everywhere we go and try to incorporate them into what we do. Why wouldn't we want to make the most of the time we have with them?

The Adventure Is Just Getting Started

D & S: The bottom line is that having kids doesn't mean your days of adventure are over. In fact, we would argue the opposite is true. Parenting is the greatest adventure you'll ever have! It's utterly unpredictable. You have no idea what's going to happen from one moment to the next, and every day presents a new challenge or surprise.

D: Remember when Canyon used to write all over his arms and legs with markers?

S: Oh my gosh, yes. At the moment, both our kids are obsessed with stickers. They put them on *everything*—in books, on their clothes, in their shoes, on *our* clothes, in *our* shoes, on the fridge, on the furniture—you name it. The one that drive us particularly crazy is when they put them on the windows of the truck.

D: No joke, those things are a nightmare to scrape off. They leave that sticky residue that gets all smeary . . .

S: The thing is, it's actually kind of cute. It has sort of become a running joke in our family. Whenever we visit Dan's parents in Wisconsin, the kids will hide stickers all over their house. When his mom and stepdad run across them, they'll send us pictures, and Canyon and Ember giggle like crazy. So, with the right attitude, even the slightly annoying stuff can be fun.

D: And sometimes, it's not so fun. Kids are forever getting sick—especially once they get into school or other situations where they're around other kids. We can't

AT THE END OF THE DAY, YOU HAVE TO ASK YOURSELF, *WHAT'S MORE IMPORTANT TO ME—MY KIDS OR MY STUFF?*

tell you how many times we've had plans upended by a rogue case of pink eye or when someone brought home a stomach bug that ended up taking out the whole family. And of course, there was the time Canyon ended up in the hospital with pneumonia. Our entire lives ground to a halt for a week while we sat by his bedside, waiting for him to turn the corner.

S: I don't think I slept four hours that week.

D: We've never loved, laughed, cried, or prayed harder than we have since welcoming Canyon and Ember into the world. Correction: since Canyon and Ember welcomed us into *their* world.

Watching your kids learn and discover and grow truly is one of the greatest adventures there is—and you don't even have to leave home to experience it (though it's a million times more fun if you do!).

Of course, the very thing that makes kids so much fun to be around is the same thing that makes them so challenging and unpredictable: they are their own people. They're not puppets on a string. You can't control their moods. They can be absolute angels one day (or hour) and complete terrors the next. One day they love doing something, and the next day they don't. There's no rhyme or reason as to why.

S: Take last summer, for example. Canyon loves going to the ocean, but one time he refused to go to the beach because he didn't want to get sand all over him. We didn't flip out. We simply redirected him.

D: It was brilliant. Sam just said, "Okay, what if instead of playing in the sand, you and Daddy just play Frisbee together?" Canyon loves playing Frisbee, so he was stoked!

S: They played Frisbee for an hour, and eventually he wandered closer to the shore to help Ember build a sandcastle. Before the morning was over, he was in the water playing with the boogie board and having the time of his life.

You have to pick your battles and be ready to pivot at a moment's notice. Dan and I have climbed sheer rock faces, gone deep-sea fishing, capsized while white water rafting, and come within fifteen yards of a wild grizzly bear mama and her cubs; yet nothing has pushed, frightened, or challenged us more than raising our two little rug rats.

Canyon and Ember weren't the end of our adventures; they were just the start of them. And we have a feeling the best is yet to come.

Having Kids
DOESN'T HAVE TO BE
the End of
Your Adventures–
IT'S POSSIBLE TO INCORPORATE
YOUR KIDS INTO WHATEVER
You Enjoy Doing.

4

GOING *Though Broke*

D: One of Sam's favorite phrases when we're getting ready to embark on a new adventure is "Are we crazy?" For example:

"Are we crazy for getting a puppy and having a baby at the same time?"

"Are we crazy for wanting to live our lives online?"

Or my personal favorite: "Are we crazy for moving halfway across the country to a superexpensive state with no money in the bank, no place to live, two full-grown dogs, and a nine-month-old?"

While conventional wisdom might say, "Yes!" Sam and I rarely subscribe to conventional wisdom. We prefer to follow God's will, which is especially awesome when you love adventure, because logic and God's will don't always line up. The amazing thing about following God's will is that when he wants you to do something, things tend to fall into place. For example, when Moses led the Israelites out of Egypt, it's estimated that there were over one million people. Think of the logistics behind leading that many people through the desert! How would they get food? How would they get water? How would they escape the greatest army on earth at the time? All these things defied logic, yet God provided a safe way out. Not only did he provide food for them in the desert, but he also led them with a pillar of fire at night and a pillar of cloud by day.

When we first got married, we were living in a two-bedroom apartment in Springfield, Missouri, and as you may have already guessed, we're not exactly what you'd call "apartment people." Sure, it's nice to be able to call someone when something breaks and have it magically repaired, and while this place did have a pool, it certainly wasn't our dream home.

So when some friends of ours got a job offer in Arkansas and asked if we'd be interested in subletting the little farmhouse they'd been renting, we were all in. This place was incredible. It was over one hundred years old and sat on eighty acres of land, with access to an additional two hundred acres, complete with ponds to fish in, wooded areas to hunt in, and miles of trails, fields, and open space to hike, explore, and go four-wheeling. As if that wasn't enough, the rent was less than half what we were paying for our apartment! The second we saw it, we could *feel* the Lord calling us there.

There was just one problem: we were only three months into a six-month lease, and in order to get out of it, we would not only have to pay the remaining three months' rent, but we'd also have to repay the promotional offer they gave us when we signed. We're talking thousands of dollars, and we were living paycheck to paycheck. We were devastated.

So, with heavy hearts, we explained the situation to the man who owned the farmhouse—a sweet man in his seventies who lived just down the road—and told him that as much as we would love to live there, we just couldn't swing it financially. But still, we couldn't shake the feeling that the Lord was calling us to this property.

That night, we sat down and prayed: "God, you know how perfect this property is for us and how much we would love to live there. You also know that we can't afford to break our lease right now. So we're putting it all in your hands. If it's your will for us to stay where we are, we understand and we trust you. But if it's your will for us to move to this farmhouse, please help us find a way to make it happen. Amen."

The next day, the owner called to tell us how much he enjoyed meeting us and that he'd discussed the situation with his wife. Since they thought we'd make good tenants, they were willing to let us move in rent-free for the first couple of months until we paid off everything we owed on our lease, after which they would raise the rent by fifty dollars a month until we paid back those first three months. We were stunned. I mean, come on—three months of free rent? Who does that?

It felt like a gift—not only from the landowner but also from the Lord, who answered in a way beyond our expectations.

Where There's a Will . . .

S: Awesome landlords aside, one of the perks of living out in the country was that we had plenty of room for Dan's toys, which was great, because Dan's toys tend to be kind of big. By the time we celebrated our second wedding anniversary, I think he'd already gone through half a dozen four-wheelers, a couple of kayaks, and—

D: Don't forget about the car Pastor Christian gave me.

S: Oh, I completely forgot about that! Quick side story . . . One day the youth pastor at our church called Dan and said, "Hey, by any chance, do you know how to break into a car?"

D: And I said, "Yeah, I break into people's cars all the time."

S: At their request—to get their keys, babe. That's kind of an important plot point.

D: Anyway, it turned out he'd locked his keys in his car—not just his house keys but the keys to the church as well. So he made me a deal: if I could get them out, I could have the car.

S: Before you get too excited, it's worth mentioning that the car didn't run. It had been giving Pastor Christian fits for months, and when it finally refused to start, he decided it was time to throw in the towel and get a new one.

IT'S NOT ABOUT WHAT *WE* WANT TO DO.
IT'S ABOUT DISCERNING WHAT *GOD* WANTS US TO DO.

D: Regardless, it took me all of thirty seconds to break in. After I gave him his keys, I called my buddy Drew, and we towed it back to the farmhouse.

S: Where it sat in the yard for two months.

D: One day Sam said, "What are you going to do with that car?"

S: He just shrugged and said, "I don't know—sell it?" And I thought, *Where is he gonna find someone willing to buy a car that doesn't run?* Fortunately for us, there are a lot of Dans out there, and within days of posting it on Facebook Marketplace, he found a buyer.

D: When the guy asked how much, I told him $500 if he could get it to run. If not, I'd let him have it for $450, and he could use the other $50 to buy a new starter. Wouldn't you know—the guy took one look at it and tapped the starter with a hammer as he turned the key in the ignition, and that old heap fired right up. Long story short, I ended up making $500 for basically slipping a coat hanger into a window and jimmying the lock.

S: But we digress. The point is, back then, Dan's Craigslist deals were like a small cottage industry. He bought, sold, and traded fishing gear, hunting gear, camping supplies, computers, canoes, ATVs—you name it. So when he called me out of the blue one day and said, "Hey, how would you feel about buying a school bus?" I wasn't the least bit surprised.

D: It was a heck of a deal. The owner was only asking $1,800 for it. So I messaged the guy and asked, "Does it run?" As soon as he said, "Yep," I made an appointment for us to see it.

S: I remember asking him, "What are we going to do with a school bus?"

"I don't know," he said. "We could chop off the back end and make a giant flatbed to haul four-wheelers around. Or we could renovate it and use it like a camper."

I had to admit, the camper idea did sound kinda fun. The next thing I knew, we were at the guy's house, and Dan was grilling him about the motor and previous owners, and climbing around the roof looking for rust. When the guy stuck the key in the ignition and it fired up on the first try, Dan was sold. The fact that we didn't actually *have* $1,800 was a technicality.

D: In our minds . . .

S: Well, *yours*.

D: Okay, in my mind, the potential far outweighed the risk. Whether we were able to fix it up or not, it was still worth at least $1,800, so worst-case scenario, we could just resell it and break even. But if we could give it a bit of a facelift, we might be able to double or even triple its value. Then we could keep it for ourselves, rent it out, or sell it for a tidy profit.

S: I called the bank, which was a little awkward, because we already had two vehicle loans out—one on Dan's truck and one on my car—and said, "So . . . random question. Dan wants to buy a school bus . . ." Then I asked for a loan. Surprisingly enough, they were open to it—not so much because they saw the genius in Dan's plan but because the guy's asking price was significantly lower than the market value of the bus. At the end of the day, the payment plan amounted to about $75 a month, which, if we could turn the bus into a camper, was totally worth it. Regardless, I remember stopping on the way home to fill the tank with gas and thinking, *What did we just do?*

D: We bought a bus, babe. Keep up. Anyway, as soon as we got it back to the farmhouse, we started working on it. All but the driver's seat and the front two bench seats

had already been removed, so most of the hard work had been done for us. I didn't really have a plan, so while Sam was scrolling through Instagram looking for inspiration, I started taking the paneling off the ceiling and the walls. Then I pulled out the flooring, and we sanded everything. Then we fixed a couple of windows that had gotten jammed. All told, we probably spent about ten days working on it—mostly on the weekends—while Canyon, who was about six months old at the time, napped.

We had no idea what we were doing, but it was a lot of fun, and we had a blast talking about all the trips we could take. We even toyed with the idea of renting it out as an Airbnb on wheels. By the time we had the interior sanded down, Sam was almost as excited about it as I was.

That's when it happened.

S: Every couple of years, I get this "feeling" that a big change is coming. I don't know if it's women's intuition, the Holy Spirit, or what, but it's unmistakable. And right about the time we finished gutting the bus, I felt it.

D: By this point, we'd been living at the farmhouse for almost three years, and truth be told, we'd started feeling a little restless. In retrospect, that might have been part of the reason we bought the bus—we just needed something fun and different to do. So when our friends Chris and Traci in Colorado invited us to come and stay with them for a week, we were all for it.

S: We've always loved Colorado. There's something about the mountains that seems to scream *adventure*. That's why we spent our honeymoon there and why we vacation there at least once a year. And that's why when Chris asked Dan, "Would you have any interest in moving here and coming to work for me?" it took him about two seconds to say, "Heck yeah!"

There was just one problem. The cost of living in Colorado was through the roof, and as it was, we were barely scraping by in Missouri. I was also nervous because moving to Colorado would mean leaving all my family in Missouri, and my mom and sister had both been incredibly helpful with Canyon. We'd also be leaving almost all our friends and our entire church community behind, so we'd essentially be starting over.

D: And broke, babe. Don't forget broke.

S: Oh, trust me, I haven't. On the other hand, we *had* been feeling restless. So, as we always try to do in situations like this, we turned it over to God.

Time to Get Out of the Boat

D: For us, obedience to God trumps everything else. Regardless of what other people think or say, we don't move forward on anything that we don't believe is God's will for us, or as Sam likes to say, we don't do anything unless we feel a peace about it.

So what does that mean exactly?

For us, it starts with committing whatever we're unsure about to prayer. The Bible tells us, "Don't worry about anything; instead, pray about everything" (Philippians 4:6, NLT). It also says, "If you believe, you will receive whatever you ask for in prayer" (Matthew 21:22). Now, that doesn't mean we just tell God what we want and he makes it happen. Prayers aren't like wishes you make before blowing out the candles, and God isn't like a genie in a lamp.

When we pray to God, we simply ask him to help us see his will for us. In other words, it's not about what *we* want to do. It's about discerning what *he* wants us to do. Sometimes God's will is crystal clear. When it came to living in the farmhouse, we were literally presented with an open door in the form of three months of free rent. But it's not always that obvious.

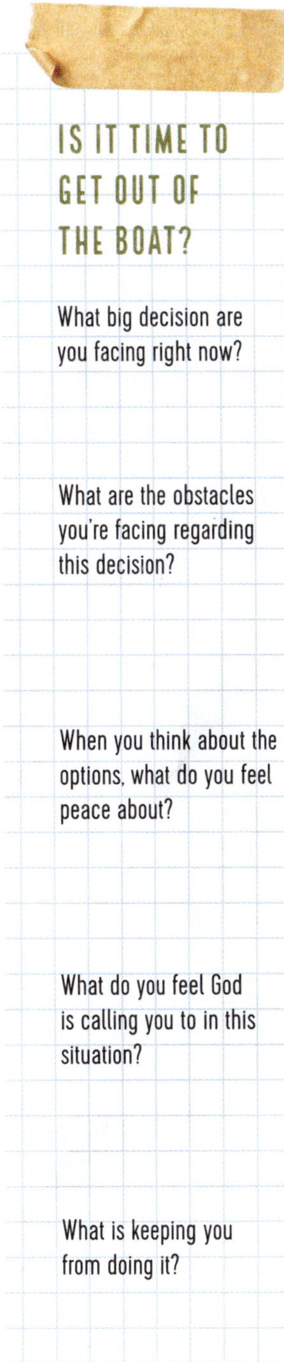

It would be great, for example, to hear the audible voice of the Lord say, "Yes, do this," or "No, don't do that," but that's not how it tends to happen. Sometimes we feel his prompting through Scripture. We'll be doing our daily reading and happen across a story or a verse that speaks directly to the situation we're in.

More often than not, though, it comes down to feeling a sense of peace about what we should do. If we pray about something and feel uneasy about it, we take that as a sign that we need to step back from whatever is in front of us for the time being.

Before we got married, I had an opportunity to serve as a youth pastor at a church in Wisconsin. Initially, everything about it seemed perfect. I had family in the area, the salary was solid—I even went out there and preached a sermon, and it went beautifully. But the more I sat with it and prayed about it, something just felt off. I couldn't explain it. I just didn't feel peace about it, so I turned it down. Well, two weeks from what would have been my start date, the senior pastor resigned. Had I taken the job, I would have been the only pastor on staff at this church, and not only was I not credentialed, I also didn't have any formal training, and I would have been in over my head. I don't know how else to explain it other than the Lord prompting me to say no for my own protection.

S: On the flip side, if we pray about a decision and we feel a sense of peace about it, we take it as a sign that the Lord wants us to act—especially if, like the farmhouse, details just start falling into place.

D: Of course, just because we feel a peace about something doesn't mean all the obstacles miraculously disappear. When we prayed about the farmhouse, for example, we didn't expect to wake up the next morning and find a sack of money sitting on the kitchen table. Even with the owner's generous offer, we were still going to have to find some way to make up the difference. Feeling God's peace doesn't eliminate all your problems; it just means you have a calmness and confidence that everything is going to be okay in spite of them.

The best way I can explain it is with a story from the Gospel of Matthew. The disciples are out on the water in the middle of the night when a terrible storm sweeps in out of nowhere. It's dark, the wind is blowing like crazy, and there are

FEELING GOD'S PEACE DOESN'T ELIMINATE ALL YOUR PROBLEMS; IT JUST MEANS YOU HAVE A CALMNESS AND CONFIDENCE THAT EVERYTHING IS GOING TO BE OKAY IN SPITE OF THEM.

massive waves threatening to capsize them at any minute. Naturally, they start to panic. Then they look out into the distance, and they see Jesus walking across the water toward them.

One of the disciples, Peter, can't believe it, so he says, "Hey, if it's really you, tell me to walk out on the water to where you are." And Jesus does. So Peter climbs over the side of the boat and starts walking across the choppy water toward Jesus.

Now, the storm doesn't go away just because Peter steps out of the boat. The wind is still blowing, and there are still waves crashing all around him. But simply knowing that Jesus is there and that he'll take care of him gives him the confidence he needs to stay afloat.

S: *That's* what we mean when we talk about feeling God's peace about something. It's not that we expect everything to turn out perfectly. We just trust that whatever does happen, as long as we continually seek his will, he'll be with us and take care of us.

So even though nothing about moving to Colorado made sense, and we had no idea how we were going to swing it financially, after committing it to prayer, we both felt a genuine peace about it.

Like we said, sometimes logic and God's will just don't line up.

D: As soon as we got back to Missouri, we started looking online for apartments in Colorado. We looked at anything and everything, even low-income apartments, but every place was unavailable, too expensive, or both. We couldn't even get past the income verification section of the applications for most places.

S: Once again, we committed it to prayer, figuring if it was the Lord's will for us to move to Colorado, a solution would present itself. The next afternoon, Dan's dad called—unsolicited—and offered to put his name on one of the applications and stay with us for a few weeks so we could claim his income. It worked, and we finally got a place. Granted, the rent was almost four times what we were paying at the farmhouse, but God had opened the door, so we walked through it.

That just left the moving expenses, and with both our parents tapped out, we weren't sure where else to turn. Then we realized the answer was sitting right in our own front yard.

Yep, you guessed it—we sold the bus. Since the loan officer at the bank had told us it was worth a lot more than what we paid for it, Dan took a chance and posted it on Facebook Marketplace for $4,000.

D: A guy from Texas messaged me almost immediately. It turns out he'd been looking for a school bus for months in hopes of doing the same thing we'd been thinking about—turning it into a camper. So we set up a video call, and I walked all around the bus, showing him all the work we'd done. Then I started it up so he could see that it ran. Two days later, he and his wife came to pick it up. He ended up haggling us down to $3,600, which was still double what we paid for it, and after paying off the bank loan, we had just enough left over to cover our moving expenses.

Now, you can call that a coincidence if you'd like, but we genuinely believe it was God's providence. For whatever reason, God seemed to be confirming our plan to go to Colorado. Granted, we still had no idea how we would afford our still-sight-unseen apartment, but as long as God kept opening doors, we were going to keep walking through them.

Leaving Your Comfort Zone in the Dust

S: Sometimes the Lord prompts us to do things, and we have no idea how it's going to work out. But *he* does. I mean, we had no idea what we were going to do with that bus when we bought it. God, however, knew exactly what lay ahead for us.

D: That's right! Our job isn't to worry about the outcome; it's simply to be obedient.

Take Abraham, for example. One day God told him, "Take your son, your only son, whom you love—Isaac—and go to the region of Moriah. Sacrifice him there as a burnt offering."

I know, right? Wondering how we would pay our rent suddenly seems like a walk in the park.

And yet Abraham did exactly as he was told. He saddled up his donkey, chopped up a bunch of wood for a fire, grabbed a couple of servants and his son Isaac, and off they went. Oh, and by the way, Moriah was a three-day trip on foot, so Abraham had *a lot* of time to think about all this.

As a father, I can't even begin to imagine what had to be going through his head during those three days. I mean, he had waited a long time for God to bless him and his wife, Sarah, with a child—one hundred years, to be exact, so he had to be wondering why God would give him a son only to turn around and take him away.

When they got to Moriah, Abraham told his servants, "Stay here with the donkey while I and the boy go over there. We will worship and then we will come back to you." Then he handed Isaac the wood and they started climbing up the side of the mountain.

Naturally, Isaac was confused. Usually, burnt sacrifices involved some kind of animal, and they didn't have any birds or sheep or goats with them. So he said to his dad, "The fire and wood are here, . . . but where is the lamb for the burnt offering?"

Abraham simply replied, "God himself will provide the lamb for the burnt offering, my son."

They made it to the top, and Abraham built an altar and arranged the wood around it for the offering. Then things got real. Abraham tied Isaac up, laid him on the altar, and picked up a knife. Just as he was about to fatally stab his only son, a voice came down from the heavens and said, "Abraham! . . . Do not lay a hand on the boy." When Abraham looked up, he saw a ram caught in a nearby thicket, which he offered as a sacrifice in Isaac's place.

LOW-COST ACTIVITIES AND HOBBIES

- playing Putt-Putt
- going to an ice cream shop
- skipping rocks
- picking wildflowers
- catching fireflies
- going on a picnic
- riding bikes
- stargazing
- having a backyard movie night
- fishing
- building forts
- donating toys to a local kids' hospital

OUR JOB ISN'T TO WORRY ABOUT THE OUTCOME; IT'S SIMPLY TO BE OBEDIENT.

Now, I don't know about you, but I'd have given anything to hear the conversation Abraham and Isaac had as they walked back down that mountain. I'm guessing the gist of it was, "Listen, son, sometimes God asks us to do hard things, and they might not always make sense. But we have to trust him and know that no matter what happens, he always has our best interests at heart."

Did Abraham know God was going to provide that ram? Honestly, I don't think so. I would guess Abraham went up there fully assuming that he was giving away the thing that meant more to him than anything else in the world. Did God know the whole time he was going to provide the ram? Definitely! But he wanted to see Abraham take that step of obedience.

Sam and I firmly believe that God wants us to step out of our comfort zone and do hard things. Being comfortable doesn't require faith. It doesn't require us to rely on God for provision. And God wants us to recognize our need for him. That's why all throughout the Bible, God is always telling his followers to "go" and "do" things they would normally never do—things they couldn't do without his help. He told five-hundred-year-old Noah to build an ark big enough to hold two of every animal that roamed the earth. He told Moses, a shepherd with questionable speaking skills, to command Pharaoh to release the Israelites from slavery. And you saw what he asked Abraham to do. None of these things were easy. Yet in each instance, God provided his people with everything they needed to accomplish what he asked them to do. He gave Noah blueprints. He parted the Red Sea so Moses and the Israelites could escape. He gave Abraham a ram.

S: And he gave us a school bus. It's not quite as dramatic, but it did show us that God had our backs—just in a slightly less Old Testamenty way.

D: That's actually a really good point.

S: Thanks, I thought so.

D: I think a big part of the reason a lot of people are afraid to step out of their comfort zone is because they don't see God working in their everyday life, and therefore, they don't believe he'll be there if they need him. But it helps to step back and remember who God is. He is the Lord of all. He created the heavens and the earth and every living thing. There is nothing happening on this earth that he is not aware of, and there is absolutely nothing he can't do.

Psalm 139 tells us,

God . . . I'm an open book to you;
even from a distance, you know what I'm thinking.
You know when I leave and when I get back;
I'm never out of your sight.
You know everything I'm going to say
before I start the first sentence.
I look behind me and you're there,
then up ahead and you're there, too—
your reassuring presence, coming and going.
This is too much, too wonderful—
I can't take it all in!

Is there anyplace I can go to avoid your Spirit?
to be out of your sight?
If I climb to the sky, you're there!
If I go underground, you're there!
If I flew on morning's wings
to the far western horizon,
You'd find me in a minute—
you're already there waiting!

Even as you read this, God is busy behind the scenes orchestrating everything. He is preparing the way for you—your next job, your next relationship, your next home, your next child, or your next adventure.

Every time you step out of your comfort zone—whether it's quitting your job to start your own business, moving to a new state, or giving the last twenty dollars in your wallet to someone on the corner in need of help even though your gas tank is on empty—you are saying to God, "I trust you. I know you are in control. And no matter what happens, I know you will always be there for me."

It's a big step, but that's what choosing adventure is all about.

More Valuable than Gold

S: When all was said and done, we ended up living in Colorado for just under two years, and it wasn't a win in the financial column. We completely drained our savings, and we had to use Dan's 401(k) to pay our bills. At one point, Dan was literally digging for change in the sofa cushions so he could buy gas.

D: It was definitely a difficult season, but we don't regret going at all. For one thing, being hundreds of miles away from our families and only knowing a handful of people in Colorado, most of whom were in a different season of life from us, meant that all we had was each other. So as a newly married couple, it brought us a lot closer.

S: On a practical level, we learned how to get by with very little, and we learned how little we really needed to get by. That's a lesson that has served us well for years.

D: No doubt. And spiritually, I can't remember a time when I felt so completely reliant upon the Lord.

S: Colorado is also where we welcomed our daughter, Ember, into our family. So even though our bank account took a significant hit, in virtually every other area of our lives, we came out ahead.

D: The funny thing is, my friends and I had been talking about moving to Colorado for years, and all my buddies were like, "Dude,

you know what's gonna happen? One of us is going to move out there, and then the rest of us will follow."

We were the first ones in our friend group to make the leap, and every couple of weeks I'd call them and say, "So when are you coming out?" And they'd be like, "Definitely next summer." But summer came and went, and it became, "Definitely this fall." Then, "Probably this spring." Pretty soon seasons turned into milestones, like, "My wife just started nursing school. We'll move out there as soon as she finishes" or, "This is home until the kids graduate."

In the end, none of them were able to make it happen.

By the time we moved back to Missouri, they were all buying houses, launching their careers, and setting up college funds for their kids; and we were basically starting over. We had one car, we were living in an old RV that was parked in a friend's driveway, and we were both looking for jobs. In fact, most of our friends seemed to feel sorry for us. We kept hearing, "Hey, guys, we're so sorry. That move really set you back."

But in our minds, moving to Colorado propelled us forward—maybe not in terms of home ownership, a healthy savings account, or a robust 401(k), but in many respects, we had spent that time investing in things that are less tangible but even more valuable to us.

In a way, our lack of material resources gave us options and a freedom that we wouldn't have had if we were tied down with careers, school, and a mortgage. It gave us a chance to move cross-country twice and experience Colorado for two years.

It all comes down to what you value the most, and Sam and I have always prioritized experiences over things. Right after high school, I took a job with a company that paid me more money per hour than I'd ever made in my life. But it came at a cost. While all my friends were enjoying their summer vacations, sleeping in, and hanging out at the lake, I was getting up 4 a.m., putting in an eight-hour day, five days a week, and then pulling a twelve-hour shift on Saturday. Sure, I made a lot of money, but I also missed out on my last summer break with my friends. I can't even remember what I bought with that money, but whatever it was, it sure wasn't worth everything I lost out on. Material possessions come and go. Memories last

forever. And for us, the memories we created in Colorado were far more valuable than any car, boat, house, or nest egg we could have acquired in that time.

That's why, to this day, whenever Sam gets one of her "something big is about to happen" feelings and asks me if we're crazy for doing something that most people would consider audacious or even ill-advised, I ask her, "Do you feel a peace about it?" And if she says, "Yep," I say, "All right then, let's do it."

And then we step out of the boat.

IF YOU WANT TO SEE

the Miracles,

YOU'VE GOT TO

Get Out of the Boat.

SEPTEMBER 2020
25 MILES NORTHEAST OF MULESHOE, COLORADO

D: You know how people talk about their life flashing before their eyes right before they think they're going to die?

Well, as I stood there staring down two potential ex-felons, all but certain they were going to kill us both and steal our truck and everything in it, I'd like to say that my first (or last) thought was of Sam or our kids, but to be brutally honest, at that moment, the only thought running through my mind was, *How can I get out of this alive?*

S: Thanks, babe. Good to hear.

D: At least you had a weapon.

S: True, but who are we kidding—if the three of you had gotten into it, with my aim, I probably would have ended up shooting you.

D: Anyway, I figured my best bet was to go into aggressor mode, so I took a deep breath and, in the most intimidating voice I could muster, said, "Hey."

S: That's tellin' 'em.

D: Would you like to tell this story?

S: Sorry, go ahead. Just forget I'm here—again.

D: (Sigh) Anyway, they just stared at me for a second, then the older guy—the one with the long chain who was covered in scars—took a few steps forward, glanced over my shoulder, smiled at Sam, then looked at me and said, "Hey. My name's Jerry. This here is my nephew, Fatty. We understand you're having a little car trouble."

Man, I exhaled so hard, I'm surprised I didn't blow them both over. "Yeah," I said, trying to sound as authoritative as possible, "I think the tensioner pulley broke off."

He nodded toward the truck. "Mind if we take a look?"

I said, "Sure" and stepped out of the way so they could open the hood. Meanwhile, Sam was sitting in the passenger seat with a solid death grip on the pistol.

They poked around the engine for a few minutes, exchanged a few words in Spanish, then Jerry nodded and said, "Yeah, it's definitely the tensioner pulley. It looks like you need a new serpentine belt too."

Sweet, I thought, *I was right.* For a guy who didn't know much about cars, I actually knew what I was talking about.

"Cool. So you guys can fix it then?" I asked.

They both looked under the hood again, then Fatty said something to Jerry in a hushed voice, and they had another brief exchange in Spanish, during which Sam and I exchanged concerned glances through the windshield.

S: All I could think was, *Great . . . now they know the truck is dead, and we're trapped here. That's it. We're history!*

D: Stay tuned for chapter 11: "How to Stay Calm in a Crisis!" Anyway, Jerry nodded and said, "Yeah, it's an easy fix. We just need to run back to the store and grab the parts."

Okay. That threw me. "You guys didn't bring the parts with you?"

Jerry shook his head. "We wanted to see what you needed first. And also . . . we'll need some money." I looked at Fatty. He just stood there quietly. I was fairly confident Fatty could easily take me in a fight. In fact, I was fairly certain both of them could.

"Yeah . . . sure," I said, slowly backing away. "Just give me a second." Then I walked over to the passenger's side window to talk to Sam.

"Hey, I've got to go with these guys to pick up the parts." She looked at me like I'd just grown a second head.

"You're not seriously getting into a car with these guys?"

"What else am I supposed to do? Give them our credit card?"

S: Okay. He had a point. Still . . . "Can't you just pay them back later?"

"With what? All I have is a twenty. The belt alone is gonna cost at least thirty."

"Babe, this isn't even our truck."

"I know, which is why you need to stay with it. You'll be fine. Just keep the doors locked, and if we're not back in half an hour, call . . ."

"Call who?"

D: Okay. Now *she* had a point. But as much as I hated the idea of leaving her there, we really didn't have any other options. "I'll be gone for fifteen or twenty minutes max. Just keep your phone on, and if I call, answer!"

S: "Fine," I said, "but you keep *your* phone on so I can follow your location."

"Deal. And don't worry—I'm sure these guys are okay."

What Dan was basing that on, I had no idea. As I watched him climb into the back seat of their truck and drive away in a cloud of dust, all I could think of were the homicide stats my mom had told me about. Suddenly, her tracking our every move from four states away didn't seem quite so paranoid.

It was starting to get chilly out, so I rolled up the windows, and after triple-checking the locks, I pulled up the tracker on my phone and watched as the little circle with Dan's picture in it moved slowly down East Fifth Street, turned left onto Main Street, then right onto West Seventh. I watched them pass a car wash, a lumberyard, someplace called Fat Fenders Roadhouse, and what looked like a combination motel-apartment complex. It wasn't until they came to a stop at O'Reilly Auto Parts that I realized I'd been holding my breath the entire time.

I checked my watch. *Okay, they left like ten minutes ago. Assuming it takes them ten minutes to pick up the parts and another ten to get back here, they should be back by 6:20, 6:30 at the absolute latest.*

I watched the little circle move almost imperceptibly through the auto parts store, then I breathed a sigh of relief when the truck pulled out of the lot and back onto West Seventh.

Okay, they're coming back. Wait . . . I zoomed out a little and double-checked the landmarks. Sure enough, they were going the wrong way on Seventh. My heart leaped into my throat. *Where are they going?*

Just then, my phone rang. It was my mom. I checked my watch again. It had been almost forty-five minutes since I'd told her the mechanic was on his way. I sent the call to voicemail and went back to tracking Dan, who had now turned onto Route 340, heading south. *Oh, gosh! Where are they taking him?*

I hit the call button. It rang six times, then went to voicemail. I called again. Same. *Why isn't he answering?* I checked the tracker again. They were still headed south and were now way off the main road.

I tried again. *Pick up, Dan!* As soon as the voicemail prompt came on, I hung up and started to text.

Are you OK? Please call me!

By this point, I was near tears. While I waited for Dan to call or text me back, I closed my eyes and threw out a quick prayer. *Please God. I don't know what's happening, but please turn that car around and bring Dan back here safely.*

As if on cue, my phone rang. My heart leaped, then sank. It was my mom again. I considered answering for a split second, then sent the call to voicemail. I felt terrible. I knew she was worried about us. So was I. But what was I going to say? *Hey, Mom. The truck we borrowed from a couple of strangers in Kansas this morning threw a tensioner pulley, and Dan just left me in the parking lot of an abandoned motel to go off with two ex-felons. One of them is covered in burns, the other one looks like he just got out of prison, and I'm fairly certain they just held up the auto parts store, kidnapped Dan, and are currently headed to the Mexican border. But don't worry, I've got a BB gun!*

Oh yeah, we were *never* going to hear the end of this.

To be continued . . .

5

KEEP *Moving Forward*

D & S: If we had a dollar for every time someone told us, "Man, I wish I could live the way you guys do," we'd probably have enough money to move back to Colorado. Then again, if we had a dollar for every time somebody online criticized our lifestyle or called us irresponsible for living the way we do, not only would we be able to move back to Colorado, we'd be able to build a lovely six-bedroom house in the foothills.

The funny thing is, when you get right down to it, both comments are essentially coming from the same place: fear. One of the main things we believe keeps people from living an adventurous lifestyle is that they're afraid to try. They're afraid it won't work out or they'll lose a ton of money. That fear holds them captive and keeps them stuck.

But if we don't push ourselves—if we don't test our limits—we'll never grow. Like a muscle that never gets stretched, we'll start to atrophy. That's why we can't let fear stop us from trying new things. The truth is, we're all capable of so much more than we give ourselves credit for. Bear Grylls, one of the greatest adventurers of all time, once said, "Whenever you do something beyond your 'comfort zone' and realize you are still standing, the more you will *believe* that the impossible is actually possible. And on the road to success, belief is everything. . . . We all have much further to push ourselves than we might initially imagine. Inside us all, just waiting to be tested, is a better, bolder, braver version of who we think we are."

The problem is, we tend to overthink things, and in our attempt to prepare for every possible eventuality, we fill our heads with so many worst-case scenarios and what-ifs that we become incapable of moving forward. But as Pastor Rick Warren writes, "Fear is always worse than reality. . . . Failure [itself] is no big deal. You just get up and start over. . . . Fear goes on for hours and days and years."

We've done a lot of wild stuff over the years, yet not one of our worst-case scenarios has come to fruition. In fact, some of our favorite adventures are those that frightened us the most at first!

Take the Next Step

S: In 2013, I had a once-in-a-lifetime opportunity to go to Israel with my sister and a couple of our friends to tour the Holy Land. It was an incredible experience. Walking where Jesus walked and seeing the places I'd been reading about in Scripture brought the Bible to life in ways I never imagined possible.

One of the coolest places we visited was the Pool of Siloam, where Jesus healed a man who was blind. In order to get to the pool, you first have to walk through something called Hezekiah's Tunnel. It's only about 1,750 feet long, but it's more than one hundred feet underground, and . . . oh, yeah, it's filled with constantly running water that comes up to your knees.

"If you're at all claustrophobic," our tour guide warned, "don't go down there. It's pitch-black and a tight fit, and it takes at least thirty minutes to make it to the other side."

Now, I wouldn't say that I'm *super* claustrophobic, but if they were selling tickets for a chance to spend thirty fun-filled minutes trapped underground in a dark, water-filled tunnel, I wouldn't exactly get in line. But when would I ever get another chance to wade in the same water that Jesus healed someone in?

So I got in line.

Right before we entered the tunnel, they gave each of us a little headlamp to wear, along with a stern warning: "Whatever you do, don't stop. Otherwise, the whole line will back up. Just keep moving. You'll eventually get to the other side."

As I took my first few steps into the darkened tunnel, I thought, *Okay, I got this.* Then, about two hundred yards in, someone stopped. I don't know if they were trying to be funny or they legit couldn't see, but I started to feel my claustrophobia well up. There we were—in the dark, standing inches apart in ice-cold, knee-deep water, with no room to pass or turn around. In the blink of an eye, I went from *I got this* to *This is it. The water is going to start rising, we're going to run out of air, and we're all going to die.*

Just as I was on the verge of a full-blown panic attack, a voice from behind me called out, "Keep moving forward!" Almost instantly, the line started moving again. Ten minutes later, we rounded a bend, and I could see daylight. As I emerged from the dark, dank tunnel and waded into the sun-kissed Pool of Siloam, my first thought was, *Okay, as scary as that was, I'm so glad I did this!*

My second thought, as I glanced to my left where a group of people were casually making their way down to the pool from a nearby road, was *Wait—we could have just gone around?*

As it turns out, yes, we could have. Later I found out there's a second tunnel that leads to the pool that is not only dry but fully lit!

Sure, both of those options would have been easier than the one I chose, but neither would have been as rewarding—or half as much fun! Plus, like Dan always says, "It's not a real adventure unless it's a little scary."

Was it scary? Yes. Was I ever in any real danger? No. We might not have been able to see the light at the end, but thanks to our little headlamps, we were able to see exactly what we needed to see.

I think it's fitting that Psalm 119 calls God's Word "a *lamp* to guide my feet," not a flashlight. While a flashlight can illuminate everything that's ahead, a lamp allows you to see only your next step, nothing more. What comes after that, only

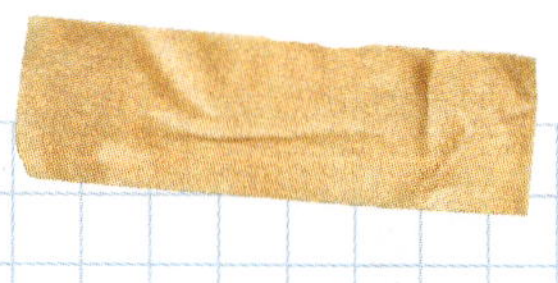

WHEN YOU'RE AFRAID, WHAT DO YOU DO?

In the story of the three servants in Matthew 25, which of the servants are you? Which one do you want to be, and why?

God knows for certain. The good news is, it's not our job to worry about the future. Our job is just to stay in his light and take that next step, then the next one, and the next one.

No Risk, No Reward

S: That's not to say that moving forward in spite of your fear is easy. I mean, that line stopped moving for all of thirty seconds, and my mind instantly went to the worst-case scenario. We all do that—it's human nature. The key to living a life of adventure is not letting the worst-case scenario keep you from taking the occasional risk. That's not irresponsible; in fact, that's exactly what God wants us to do.

There's a great story in the Gospel of Matthew that sums this up beautifully. It's about a wealthy businessman who is getting ready to go on a trip. Before he leaves, he calls three of his servants and gives each of them some money to take care of while he's away. He gives the first one $5,000; he gives the second one $2,000; and he gives the third one $1,000.

As soon as the businessman leaves, the first servant invests the money he was given and doubles it, as does the second servant. But the third servant is terrified of losing any of his boss's money, so he locks up his share in a safe.

When the businessman gets back, he calls his servants together again and asks them what they did with his money. The first one says, "I invested your money and doubled it!" To which the businessman says, "Excellent! Come see me tomorrow, and I'll give you more to invest!"

Then the second servant tells him he has also doubled the money he was given, to which the businessman says, "Excellent! Come see me tomorrow, and I'll give you more to invest as well!"

Then the third servant says, "Yeah, I was of afraid of losing the money you gave me, so as soon as you left, I put it in the safe." He then hands over the original $1,000 he was given.

IF WE DON'T PUSH OURSELVES—
IF WE DON'T TEST OUR LIMITS—WE'LL NEVER GROW.

Well, the businessman is furious. He shouts, "That's a terrible way to live! It's criminal to live cautiously like that!" (Matthew 25:26, MSG). Then he gives the third servant's $1,000 to the first servant and throws the third servant out of the house.

You see? God doesn't want us to let fear hold us captive. He invites us—and expects us—to take chances, step out in faith, and live life to the fullest.

There's an old saying that if a captain's number one priority was to make sure his ship was safe, he would just keep it tied up to the dock forever. But that's not what ships are made for. Ships are made to sail the open seas! Sure, never leaving the dock exponentially reduces the possibility of sinking, being attacked by sharks, or getting caught in unexpected storms. But what's the point of owning a boat if you never take it out on the water?

D: Babe, we should totally get a boat.

S: Stick with me here. It's like those guys who spend a fortune on action figures but never take them out of the original packaging for fear of reducing their value. Action figures aren't made to be looked at through a plastic wrapper. They're made to be played with (the word *action* is literally in the name!). Their real value lies in the enjoyment you get from playing with them, not from keeping them in pristine condition to maybe sell somewhere down the line. Our kids have broken more than their fair share of toys, but we accept that as a possibility going in. We don't encourage it—I mean, some of those toys are expensive. But we'd rather the toys get broken because they've been played with too hard than have our kids be so terrified of breaking something that they never take their toys out of the box.

D: Better yet, picture your favorite shirt or sweater. You probably wear it a lot, right? Of course you do, because you love it! Sam has an oversized sweatshirt that she wears four or five days a week. She has spilled coffee on it, wiped Cheetos dust on it, walked the dog in it, slept in it, run errands in it, worked out in it—I swear, most days that mangy thing could probably walk around the house by itself. You know what she doesn't do with it? Keep it buried away at the bottom of a drawer or her closet so it stays in like-new condition. Someday she's going to pull that thing out of the dryer and it will disintegrate in her hands. And when it does, we will gather around the tattered remnants as a family and say, "Well done, good and faithful sweatshirt—you lived your life to the fullest." We should all aspire to live like Sam's sweatshirt!

S: Okay, Dan has gone off the rails a little here, but his point is valid. Just as boats are made to be taken out on the water, toys are made to be played with, and our favorite clothes are made to be worn, we were made to live life to the fullest. God created the world for us to enjoy. And he wants us to enjoy it! Why else would he create mountains and oceans and forests and canyons and deserts if he didn't intend for us to explore them? And why else would he fill the world with thousands of different birds, trees, flowers, fish, animals, foods, sights, sounds, and smells if he didn't want us to experience them?

And if something bad *does* happen, that doesn't mean it's the end of the world.

S: In 2019, Dan and I got to take the trip of a lifetime to Kodiak, Alaska. Like most of our adventures, it kind of came about by accident. I was poking around on Instagram, and I happened upon a bunch of pictures posted by a friend of mine who had recently moved to Alaska with her husband. Their new house was surrounded by mountains, with the coastline nearby, and it looked absolutely stunning. I shot her a quick text to reconnect and tell her how beautiful her shots were. She said, "Anytime you and Dan want to come out, you've got a free place to stay!"

As attractive as the offer was, we were still living in Colorado and were beyond flat broke, so even with a free place to stay, there was no way we could pull it off.

However, when my mom offered to not only pay our airfare but also come out and watch the kids for us as a belated fifth anniversary gift, we thought, *Well, hey—this clearly seems like a sign!* So we packed up all Dan's hunting stuff, set our financial problems on the back burner for a few days, and flew to Anchorage.

D: It was awesome—like Colorado on steroids! Between the mountains, the wilderness, and the ocean, literally every view was like a picture on a postcard. On our first day there, we went for a hike up the side of a mountain, and on the way up, we helped ourselves to hundreds of wild blueberries and salmonberries lining the path in thickets nine feet tall and ten feet deep. They were so delicious, they didn't even seem real—and they were everywhere! At one point, I turned to Sam and said, "Can you believe this? It's like we're living in the land of milk and honey. Almost everything we need is literally at our feet and free for the taking." No joke—it felt like we were in heaven. And then it got even better.

The next day, Sam's friends took us out on the ocean to go fishing. It was unreal—we saw bald eagles flying overhead, and sea lions, jellyfish, and sea otters circling our boat. Just when we thought it couldn't get any cooler, a massive humpback whale leaped up out of the water, rolled onto its side, and splashed back down not forty yards from us. Sam and I almost lost our ever-loving minds! I don't think I cast my line once the entire time we were out there. I was too busy staring, slack-jawed, at the wonder of nature on display right in front of us.

S: It really was incredible. You almost hated to blink for fear you'd miss something. Suddenly a week didn't seem like nearly enough time. I couldn't see how we would be able to take it all in.

GOD DOESN'T WANT US TO LET FEAR HOLD US CAPTIVE. HE INVITES US—AND EXPECTS US—TO TAKE CHANCES, STEP OUT IN FAITH, AND LIVE LIFE TO THE FULLEST.

D: Wanting to make the most of every minute, Sam and I got up extra early the next morning to sneak in a quick hike before going fly-fishing. Then Sam's mom called.

"Hey," she said, kind of sheepishly. "I'm not quite sure how to tell you this, but . . . someone stole your truck."

"Seriously? Somebody stole the Denali?"

"I'm so sorry," she said. "It was in the parking lot last night, but when I went out this morning, it was gone."

"Did you call the police?" Dan asked.

"I did."

"Did you file a report?"

"Yes."

S: We just stared at each other for a second, then Dan said, "Well, you've still got Sam's car, so you can use that until we get home. Keep us posted, and let us know if you hear anything from the police."

My mom was silent on the other end, then said, "So . . . you're . . . what are you two going to do?"

Dan just shrugged. "We're going for a hike, then we're gonna go fly-fishing. Oh, and unless you moved them for some reason, you'll need to pick up some new car seats. They were in the truck."

Mom waited another beat, then said, "Seriously?"

I know, I know—having your car stolen is a pretty big deal, especially when you're already in the hole financially. And yes, in case you're wondering, that was my "pride and joy" Denali—the one Canyon all but ruined with the rocks.

D: Face it, babe, the truck was cursed. And sure, we could have spent the whole day sitting around wringing our hands, talking to the insurance company, and worrying about how much it would cost to get a new truck and replace the car seats, power tools, and camping gear that were inside. We could have said, "We've got to go home and deal with this" and flown back home. But what would that have accomplished? The truck was gone. Robin had already called the police and filed a report. There really wasn't anything else we could do. Worrying about it wasn't going to help. Besides, we were having the time of our lives. The dude had already stolen our Denali. We weren't going to let him ruin the vacation of a lifetime too.

Spinning Your Wheels

S: Dan rarely worries about anything, but when we first got married, I worried a lot—especially about money. Growing up with a single mom, there were always concerns about being able to pay the bills, so worrying was just something that came naturally to me. Even now, I often find myself worrying about the kids, about money, and about the future. But as Dan always reminds me, worrying is just our way of telling God he's not big enough.

In the Gospel of Luke, Jesus tells his disciples, "Do not worry about your life, what you will eat; or about your body, what you will wear. For life is more than food, and the body more than clothes. Consider the ravens: They do not sow or reap, they have no storeroom or barn; yet God feeds them. And how much more valuable you are than birds! Who of you by worrying can add a single hour to your life?" I love that passage, because it's a great reminder that worrying isn't the answer—*and* that God is looking out for us!

D: God doesn't want us to spend our lives worrying. He wants us to spend our lives *living*! All worrying does is steal our joy and rob us of time and energy we can't get back.

We can't always control what happens to us, but we *can* control how we react to it. We can let it bring us down, set us

AN ADVENTURER'S CHECKLIST

If you could bring only five things in your backpack, what would you bring to survive on a wilderness hike?

- ☐ flashlight
- ☐ fire starter
- ☐ Swiss Army Knife
- ☐ rope
- ☐ compass
- ☐ map
- ☐ walkie-talkie
- ☐ bear spray
- ☐ emergency whistle
- ☐ flares
- ☐ water
- ☐ water filter
- ☐ freeze-dried food
- ☐ first aid kit

back, and take us out of the game, or we can do what God tells us to do and cast all our anxiety on him.

S: It's not often that someone offers to deal with your problems so you don't have to. I mean, I could grow old and gray waiting for Dan to scrub out a toilet or volunteer to cook dinner every once in a while. Yet God offers to carry our burdens for us every minute of every day. We only have to ask.

That's why now, whenever I feel myself starting to worry or obsess over something I have no control over, I stop what I'm doing, take a deep breath, and pray. I might not always have the right words, but the sheer act of praying momentarily takes my mind off whatever I'm worrying about and focuses my attention on God—and sometimes that's enough to give me the clarity I'm lacking.

D: Did it suck that our truck got stolen? You bet it did! Sam loved that truck! But it wasn't the end of the world. No one was hurt. We were okay. The kids were okay. And Sam's mom was okay. The only way our stolen truck was going to ruin our vacation was if we let it. And we had no intention of letting that happen.

D: After we got off the phone with Sam's mom, we went out for a hike, as planned, and picked two giant buckets of salmonberries that we ended up vacuum-sealing and bringing home with us. Then we met up with our friends to go fly-fishing.

Now, I've been fly-fishing loads of times, but I'd never seen anything like this before. There were massive schools of salmon swimming from one tide pool to the next, and the water was so crystal clear, I felt like I could almost reach right in and grab one.

The best part, though? As we were getting our gear ready, I heard a branch snap across the river, and when I looked up, I saw two full-grown grizzly bears walking along the shoreline on the other side, not twenty feet away from us.

Before we'd gone out that morning, Sam's friends had schooled us on what to do if we encountered a bear. "If you see a bear, whatever you do, don't run," they told us. "It will chase after you, and there's no way you'll outrun it. Just slowly back away, and if it keeps following you, use your bear spray."

By the way, if you're not familiar with it, bear spray is basically red pepper oil in aerosol form. The idea is to spray it in the bear's face—kind of like mace—to blind it long enough for you to get away. Nobody goes hunting, fishing, hiking, or camping in Alaska without it.

Anyway, Sam's friend also saw the bears, and, being a local, she said calmly and quietly, "Everybody slowly back away from the river."

I looked across the river at the bears, then down at the salmon swimming past my feet and thought, *Are you kidding me? Look at all these fish!*

Then one of the bears looked right at us and stepped into the river.

The next thing I knew, Sam's friend whipped out her bear spray, pulled out the pin like a grenade, and, without breaking eye contact with the bear, said, "Get to the trail. Don't run but move with purpose."

The next sound I heard was Sam frantically—

S: Purposefully, babe.

D: Sorry, *purposefully* bushwhacking her way through the woods. I crouched down and started picking up all the stuff Sam had dropped before she *purposefully* fled the scene, keeping a watchful eye on the bears the entire time.

All of a sudden, one of the bears plunged its head into the water and came back out with a giant salmon in its teeth. I looked over at Sam's friend and said, "Now *that* is the coolest thing I've ever seen," to which she promptly replied, "Get to the trail, Dan—now!"

We ended up moving a little farther down the river and managed to snag enough salmon to feed all four of us that night. I have to say, although neither of us is a huge

fish fan, that was one of the best meals we've ever eaten. We even vacuum-sealed some of the extra fillets and shipped them home.

S: The next day, we did a little more fly-fishing, then Dan gathered all his hunting stuff, our two-person tent, and our sleeping bags, and we hiked up the side of a mountain and made camp. It was spectacular. There wasn't a paved road or man-made structure for miles—just trees, mountains, and blue sky as far as the eye could see. Had we brought the kids with us, we probably would have stayed in that spot forever. Seriously, Dan was in heaven.

D: Oh, 100 percent. Before we left, I'd done some research and found out that there is a certain kind of deer that can only be found in Alaska and is widely regarded as some of the best-tasting deer meat on earth. Nothing screamed adventure to me more than hiking miles into Alaska's backcountry with my head on a constant swivel and a rifle in my hand in the event that we encountered a grizzly. Just being out there was the experience of a lifetime. Still, I was hoping we'd run across at least one of those deer before we had to leave.

S: We didn't just run across *one* of them. When we crawled out of our tent the next morning, dozens of them were grazing in the clearing all around us. I had never seen anything like it. By the time lunch rolled around, we had already processed the meat to ship it back to Missouri, cleaned up our campsite, and made our way back down the mountain.

D: We spent the next three days sightseeing, hiking, biking, and paddleboarding in the ocean. By the time we left, we had vacuum-sealed and shipped home enough deer meat, berries, and salmon

fillets to last us well into the winter. It was, by far, the greatest trip we'd ever taken—and the very best of it came after one of the worst things that could have happened.

S: By the way, the police ended up finding our Denali in Nebraska. It was in pretty bad shape, and we ended up totaling it and getting another truck with the insurance money. But honestly, we'd have traded that Denali in a heartbeat for the experiences we had in Alaska. Vehicles come and go, but the memories we made that week will last us a lifetime. All we had to do was cast our worries on the Lord and keep moving forward.

Stick to the Marked Path

D: It's one thing to embrace a life of adventure and move forward with purpose like Sam did in Hezekiah's Tunnel and *almost* did when the grizzly bears appeared . . .

S: Hey, they were big bears.

D: I know, but there's a reason they tell you not to run.

S: Listen, I didn't have to outrun the bears. I only had to outrun you.

D: Oh sure, like *that* was gonna happen. Anyway, as I was saying . . . It's one thing to move forward with purpose, but it's another to rush headlong into a potentially dangerous situation haphazardly.

When I was in college, a bunch of my buddies and I went to Arkansas to spend the weekend hiking and camping along the Buffalo National River. The trail we were planning to take was pretty intense, but we were all seasoned outdoorsmen who had done a lot of overnight camping and hunting trips—all except our friend Steven.[1] When he asked if he could go along, I said, "I don't know, man. It's a really hard trail. Are you sure?"

But he was determined. "I've got this. I have a sleeping bag and a backpack and all that stuff."

---

1 Let the record state that Steven and I are still friends. He even joined our podcast to tell his version of the story!

I'll admit, I was dubious. I mean, Steven was awesome, but he never really struck me as the type of guy who'd flourish in the wild. He just didn't have much of a baseline of experience to build on. But I didn't want to discourage him, so I said, "Sure. You can come."

That was my first mistake.

Steven rushed home, and about an hour later, he showed up in a pair of old tennis shoes with a little JanSport backpack and a massive sleeping bag—still in the plastic bag, fresh off the shelf from Walmart.

I stood there in my hiking boots and waterproof backpack, which contained a change of socks, a rain jacket, a headlamp, a first aid kit, a multi-tool knife, sunscreen, matches, a lightweight hammock, a water bottle, protein bars, a flashlight, and a tightly rolled ultralightweight thermal sleeping bag designed specifically for backcountry hiking and camping. As I looked at Steven, only one thought came to mind: *This is not going to end well.*

We weren't two hundred yards down the trail when Steven wheezed, "Man, you weren't joking about this hike."

"Pace yourself," I told him. "We still have several miles of trail ahead of us, and we haven't even gotten to the hard parts yet."

To his credit, Steven did a halfway decent job keeping pace with the rest of us. It helped that we were mostly going downhill at that point and I'd volunteered to carry his sleeping bag after he dropped it and almost tripped over it a half dozen times. All of us were pretty patient until he groaned, "Aw, man . . . my water bottle is gone. I must have dropped it somewhere."

"Seriously, dude?" I said, trying not to sound as exasperated as I felt.

He shrugged. "It's a tough hike."

"This is nothing," I said. "Wait till we hike back out. It's all uphill. Here," I said, handing him my water bottle. "You can share mine till we get to the campsite."

Steven spent the bulk of the following day resting at camp and tending to his blistered feet while the rest of us explored the nearby caves and waterfalls.

The next morning, over breakfast, he said, "Hey, I think I'm going to head out a few hours before you guys. It's going to take me a lot longer to hike back up to the trailhead, and I don't want to slow you down."

On the one hand, it made sense. At the pace Steven walked, even if he left a full hour before us, we'd probably catch up with him in no time. But given all the help he'd needed hiking in, what were the odds he'd be okay hiking back out on his own?

"Are you sure?" I asked.

"Positive," he said.

I looked at the other guys, and they just shrugged.

"Okay, then," I told him. "Just follow the footpath till you reach the river crossing, then turn left at the post marker and follow the trail out the rest of the way. We'll catch up to you as soon as we can."

That was my second mistake.

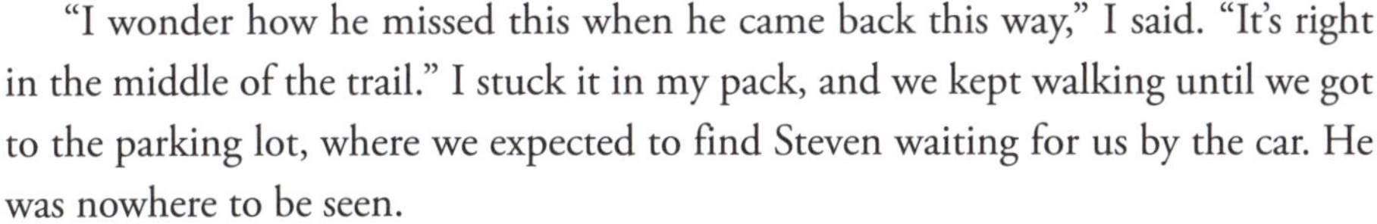

After Steven left, we spent some more time exploring the area and doing a little cliff diving into the river near one of the trails. After a few hours, we decided to pack up camp and start heading back.

When we got to the river crossing, we spotted the bright green water bottle Steven had dropped on the way down.

"I wonder how he missed this when he came back this way," I said. "It's right in the middle of the trail." I stuck it in my pack, and we kept walking until we got to the parking lot, where we expected to find Steven waiting for us by the car. He was nowhere to be seen.

"Where is he?" I asked.

"You don't think he got lost, do you?" one of my buddies asked.

"The directions were pretty simple," I said. "There's just one well-marked turn after you cross the river, then it's a straight shot all the way."

"But we found his water bottle *before* the river crossing," one of them pointed out. "What if he didn't come that way?"

I dug my phone out of my backpack. I only had one bar. We tried calling Steven, but it kept going straight to voicemail. Our best guess was that he was at the bottom of a canyon with no service.

I looked back toward the gorge and scanned the horizon. There were thousands of acres of wilderness surrounding the river. "If he turned off the trail before he got to the river . . ." My stomach sank. *He could be anywhere.*

This was not good.

I looked at my watch. "Okay, we have maybe forty-five minutes of daylight left, tops. He's been walking for at least four hours, he doesn't have a water bottle with him, and we have no idea where he got off the trail."

My mind was racing. *Why did I let him go off on his own this morning?*

I took a deep breath and turned to my friends. "All right, everyone, lighten your pack. Make sure you have enough food and water to get you through the night, and bring your headlamp. Here's what we're going to do. Brad, you take the car and drive to the trailhead on the other side of the canyon. If Steven got turned around leaving camp, he might have ended up there. Jake and Phil, you take the other path down to the river in case he crossed someplace else and accidentally turned right instead of left at the post. Jimmy and I will take the long trail back to the campsite. As long as he's on one of the marked trails or paths, we should find him.

"Do you think we should call somebody back at the school to let them know Steven is lost?" Brad asked.

I hated to do that, especially since I fully expected to find him any minute. But I knew Brad was right. "Yeah . . . probably." At that point, it was a toss-up as to who I was more upset with: Steven for getting lost or myself for letting him come in the first place.

Trying to stay calm, I called the president of the college. There was no answer, so I left a voicemail. "Hey, this is Dan Mathews. I'm calling from Buffalo National River Park, and we can't find Steven. Phil, Brad, Jake, Jimmy, and I are all heading out now to look for him, but we wanted to make sure you knew."

Well, that shouldn't send anyone into a blind panic, I thought, shoving the phone back into my pack.

We spent the next six hours running up and down every trail in the area, calling out for Steven and getting no response. But when we got back to the river, we found a pair of Steven's socks, soaking wet, draped over a log.

"Okay," I said, feeling a faint sliver of hope, "he's got to be in this general area."

We called Steven's name several times, but there was still no answer. Then we saw a light coming toward us down the trail.

That's gotta be him, I thought. Who else would still be out on the trail this late?

Our hearts sank as two park rangers emerged from the darkness. One of them shone his flashlight at us and said, "We're looking for a missing hiker named Steven."

I shaded my eyes from the glare. "So are we. We're the group that was with him."

"Where did you last see him?" the second ranger asked, pulling out a map. I pointed out the campsite and traced the path I had told Steven to take. I also showed him where we found his socks and water bottle, as well as the trails we had already covered.

"Okay," the lead ranger said, folding up the map. "We already have three two-man teams searching for him, so why don't you guys head back to the trailhead. If we haven't found him by morning, you can join in the search again."

As much as I hated to give up, I could see their point. It was late, it had been a stressful afternoon, and we were exhausted. The last thing they needed was for us to get lost too. So, feeling completely dejected, we started back toward the parking lot.

It wasn't long before we saw another flashlight beam coming toward us.

"Steven?" Phil called. "Is that you?"

It was the president of our college and the dean of students. They had driven down after hearing my message and had been searching for him for almost an hour. They were also the ones who had called the park rangers.

If you're keeping score, that's five teams of people all wandering around in the dark looking for Steven. At that point, it might have been easier if Steven had been out looking for us.

"What were you thinking?" the president half-shouted at us. "How could you let Steven wander around out here by himself?"

"Well . . ." Before I could answer, he cut me off. "Turn around! We're not leaving here until we find him."

"But the rangers told us to go back to the parking lot," Jimmy said.

"That's right," I put in. "They said we should wait at the trailhead, and if they haven't found him by morning, we can keep looking."

They didn't look at all pleased, but they did concede that we should all head back. It took us roughly an hour to get back to the trailhead, and aside from occasionally

DON'T LET FEAR OR A SETBACK STOP YOU FROM ENJOYING LIFE TO THE FULLEST.

shouting Steven's name into the darkness, nobody said a word. It was late, we were exhausted, and the temperature was dropping quickly.

The next morning, before sunrise, the president and the dean were waiting for us with coffee and breakfast, and we all set out together to look for Steven. At one point, we bumped into one of the teams of park rangers who had been out searching all night, but there was still no sign of Steven. After hours of fruitless searching, we made our way back up the trail to grab a bite to eat before setting back out again.

When we got within a hundred yards of the trailhead, our cell service came back, and our phones started pinging as a series of texts from other students at school popped up, one after another:

Praise the Lord! They found Steven!

He's safe! Praise God!

He once was lost, but now he's found!

Sure enough, when we got back to the parking lot, there was Steven, sitting on the back of a fire truck, wrapped in a reflective emergency blanket, with a big smile on his face, eating an MRE.

How he managed to stumble out of those woods undetected despite every path and trail crawling with rescuers I'll never know, but I *can* tell you this: it's been over a decade now, and I still kick myself for letting Steven walk into a situation where he was clearly in over his head. It was irresponsible on my part and downright reckless on his.

I learned an important lesson that day, and now I am careful to make sure everyone in the group is prepared for the adventure ahead. As for Steven, I'm pretty sure he has retired that old backpack!

Walk before You Run

D: Stepping out of your comfort zone is one thing, but had Sam been severely claustrophobic, going down into Hezekiah's Tunnel wouldn't have been adventurous; it would have been reckless. Had she

panicked and tried to force her way out, other people could have been seriously hurt.

Yes, God tells us to go, to see new places, to meet new people, and to try new things. But we need to be responsible with how we do that.

I think Bear Grylls was spot-on when he said, "Adventure should be 80 percent 'I think this is manageable,' but it's good to have that last 20 percent where you're right outside your comfort zone. Still safe, but outside your comfort zone."

So how do you differentiate between a calculated risk and reckless or irresponsible behavior? You've probably heard the expression "You have to walk before you can run." Well, that's a great piece of advice. Start small and work your way up. If you've never tried rock climbing before, don't start with El Capitan. Go to one of those climbing centers where you can practice on a climbing wall on a belay, so even if you fall, you won't get hurt. Never been kayaking before? Take a class at the YMCA with certified instructors in a swimming pool before you head out onto the open sea or decide to try shooting the rapids with your friends.

Remember, the whole point of choosing adventure is simply to try something new—not to get hurt! Pitching a tent and camping out with the kids can be just as much fun in your own backyard as it is at Yellowstone—not to mention a whole lot safer, especially if you've never done it before.

S: Speaking of which, it's okay to admit that you don't know what you're doing. Part of choosing adventure is learning new skills. Before I met Dan, I had never been backpacking in the woods, I'd never been rock climbing—I'd never even tried cheese curds (there's just something about the word *curds* that sounds unappealing). But I leaned into his expertise, we took it one step—and curd!—at a time, and eventually, I learned to love all three.

So, go! Do something new, travel to a new place, meet new people, experience new things—but take it one step at a time.

Don't let fear or a setback stop you from enjoying life to the fullest. Just keep moving forward, one step at a time. We promise you'll be thankful you did.

LIVING A LIFE OF

Adventure

DOESN'T MEAN ACTING RECKLESSLY.

WHEN IN DOUBT,

Keep Moving Forward.

MOVE WITH PURPOSE,

AND WALK BEFORE YOU TRY TO RUN.

6

THERE HAS TO BE *More to Life*

S: Here's the thing about being pregnant—the first nine months are awesome! You're growing another human being, your body is changing every day, and there's an ever-present feeling of excitement and anticipation that just keeps building. Then you give birth. This is where we failed to really think the whole "let's have a baby every eighteen months" thing through.

We had Canyon at the end of August, so we still had several months of warm weather when we could get out of the house and go hiking and climbing and exploring, which was incredibly therapeutic. We also had Canyon in Missouri, surrounded by family and friends.

But we had Ember in March, when the weather was downright miserable. It was cold, and there was about a foot of snow on the ground. Plus, we were in Colorado with no real community to lean on. With Dan away at work all day, I was stuck in our dungeon of an apartment with no natural light, an eighteen-month-old, a newborn, and a nasty case of mastitis. That made for one rough postpartum journey.

It was the same thing every day: get up, change the kids, feed the kids, naptime, feed them again, change them again, bathtime, put them down—over and over and over. I lived for evenings and weekends, because then at least Dan was home, and I had someone to talk to who could actually talk back. But for the most part, one day just bled into the next.

I was desperate to find some kind of creative outlet. One afternoon, after I got the kids down for a nap, I was scrolling through Instagram looking for fun crafting ideas and ran across some of the old bus and RV life accounts I'd started following after Dan bought the school bus.

Prior to that little impulse buy, I had no idea these groups even existed. But once I started googling "bus renovation ideas," I stumbled onto an entire community of people who live on the road full-time in converted buses, RVs, and vans. Their pages were littered with pictures from the Grand Canyon, Yosemite, Yellowstone, Niagara Falls, the Ozarks, and all over the Pacific Northwest. The more I scrolled, the more obsessed I became with the idea of living on the road full-time.

It looked so appealing. I loved the simplicity—not having a lot of stuff, being able to travel, spending time with your family. It looked adventurous and exciting too. Then we sold the bus, moved to Colorado, had another baby, and I kind of forgot about the idea—until now.

(Warning: role reversal ahead!)

D: I had barely walked through the door that night when Sam hit me with "Hey, babe, what would you think about buying an RV?"

And before I could even answer, she said, "Because I found one online, and I want to go take a look at it."

I gotta be honest . . . this felt like it came out of nowhere, and financially, we weren't in a position to be looking at a major purchase. So I asked her, "What would we even do with an RV?"

S: First off, what *couldn't* we do? But for the sake of this argument, I said, "We could live in it! They're basically apartments on wheels, and we both hate this place. I've been looking at RV life accounts on Instagram all day, and it looks so awesome! We could go anywhere we wanted—we could *live* anywhere we wanted! It would be like camping, only more permanent. We could find a great spot on the edge of a lake

CHOOSING ADVENTURE AND CHASING ADVENTURE ARE TWO DIFFERENT THINGS.

out in the woods somewhere and live off the land. You could go out hunting every day, we could cook out over an open fire every night, and—"

D: "Wait a minute." Sam was totally wound up about this. And while she did make a lot of good—no, excellent—points, as cramped as our current apartment was, I just couldn't imagine living in an even smaller space full-time, with two kids. "Have you run the numbers on any of this?"

S: Wouldn't you know, Dan picked *that* moment to suddenly care about money. Fortunately, I was ready. "Yeah . . . actually, I have."

D: "And?"

S: "Most of the campsites in the Denver area run about $1,200 a month."

D: "Which is basically what we're paying for rent."

S: "See? Even steven."

D: I love Sam's math. "What about the cost of the RV?"

S: "It's only $7,000."

D: "Babe—"

S: "Before you say no . . . remember the bus?"

D: "Yeah, but the bus was only $1,800."

S: Just between you and me, I knew he was going to say that. I didn't marry this guy yesterday. So I quickly switched tactics to Plan B. "Exactly. And you sold it for double that—with virtually no improvements. All you did was gut it."

D: "I could have finished it if I'd wanted to . . ."

S: Now I had him. "I *know* you could have. And just imagine what you could have sold it for if we'd had time to fix it up! We might have been able to get seven, maybe eight thousand." I could see the wheels starting to turn in Dan's head, so I went in for the kill. "Okay, so maybe we can't afford to live in it, but we could still buy it, renovate it, and then rent it out on the weekends when we're not using it—kind of like an Airbnb."

D: Now *that* made sense. As long as we didn't spend a fortune on the reno, we could probably make our money back within a couple of months on out-of-towners who wanted to experience the mountains on the cheap. Whatever we made after that would be supplemental income—and man, could we have used a few extra bucks. So we made an appointment to look at the camper Sam had found.

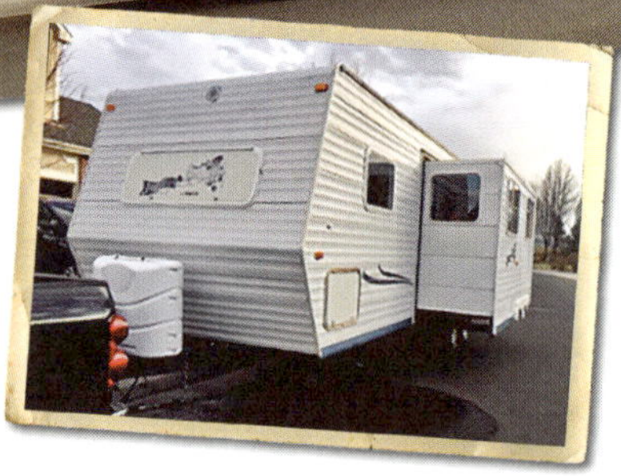

S: As soon as I saw it, I fell in love. It was a twenty-two-foot-long 2002 Jayco Jay Flight travel trailer with a slide-out dinette, two bunk beds, a small kitchen, a bathroom, and a master bedroom with a queen bed and two little end tables. The interior looked a little dated, but it had everything you'd need for a fun weekend getaway—a microwave, a stove, a small refrigerator, and hookups for gas, electric, and water.

D: I wouldn't say I fell in love with it, but as soon as I saw Sam's face, I knew we'd just bought ourselves an RV. The couple selling it had inherited it from the wife's parents, who had only used it a handful of times, so it was in great shape, and as far as I could tell, everything worked. Like Sam said, it just needed a good makeover. The next morning, after Sam called the bank, we wrote the couple a check, towed the trailer home, and parked it in the lot of the storage facility across from our apartment complex.

S: Now it was time to get to work.

Farmhouse on Wheels

D: I should start off by saying that we really didn't have a plan.

S: Oh, I definitely had a plan! The farmhouse look was super trendy at the time, so I planned to Joanna Gaines the heck out of that thing!

Because it was such a small space, I wanted everything to be a crisp, clean white—the cabinets, the walls, the ceiling, the backsplash—everything. I wanted to put shiplap up on the walls and complement that with dark woodgrain laminate flooring and oil-rubbed bronze fixtures. I'd seen hundreds of pictures online, so I knew that if we did this right, we could make this little trailer look exactly like a house.

But first, we had to get rid of the existing 1980s honey oak cabinetry, peel-and-stick marble tile floors, and floral wallpaper. And if there's one thing Dan loves doing, it's demolition.

D: I just started ripping stuff out—cabinets, flooring, wallpaper. If it wasn't nailed down, it was gone. Even if it *was* nailed down, it was gone. And I have to admit, it felt great to fire up the old power tools and get my hands dirty.

S: We had an absolute blast. Every day while the kids napped, I would scroll through Instagram looking for decorating ideas, and as soon as Dan got home, we would bundle Canyon and Ember up and head to the storage facility.

D: The vehicle was big enough that we could corral the kids on one side of the RV with a baby gate while we worked on the other side. Canyon was pretty good at keeping himself amused, and whenever Ember got fussy, I'd just hold her in my left arm and pry or drill something with my right. And for the most part, it all went pretty smoothly—except the paint.

S: At first, we were going to use rollers and brushes, but then I kept seeing all these people on Instagram using sprayers, and that looked much faster and easier.

D: To save a little money, I borrowed a sprayer from a friend at work. The only problem was that it didn't work. It turned out his wife had never cleaned the nozzle, so it had several years' worth of dried-up paint clumped inside, clogging it up.

S: In order to fix it, we had to take the whole thing apart and soak the pieces in acetone. Since that was going to take a while, we decided to go ahead and put down the new flooring—*before* we painted. That meant we were constantly dripping white paint all over the dark brown floors.

D: Actually, I wasn't even thinking about the floors. I was thinking about the weather. It turns out paint takes a long time to dry when it's cold, and it was still in the upper thirties to low forties outside, so the walls stayed tacky for days.

S: Plus, we were worried that shiplap might be too heavy, so we opted for one-quarter-inch paint-ready plywood, which soaked up the paint like a sponge.

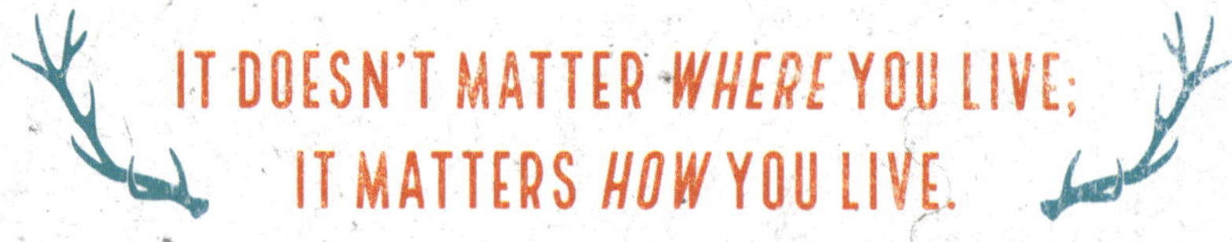

D: I've never seen anything like it. The paint went on bright white, but within a few minutes, it faded to chalky gray. We had to paint the whole interior three times. The entire trailer was less than three hundred square feet, and we ended up using almost six gallons of paint.

S: But when we finished, it looked spectacular—like something straight out of the pages of the *Magnolia* magazine. I even brought in a bunch of baskets, pillows, and wall decor that my sister and I picked up at the Silos.

D: I have to admit, for two people who had no idea what they were doing, we did a pretty good job.

S: In fact, we did such a good job, we had an offer to rent it out before we even had the water hooked up!

D: Man, that was a mess. There was a leak somewhere in the water line, and I was still trying to track it down when a couple reached out to Sam online looking for a place to stay while they were in town visiting family. We told them the RV wasn't finished yet, but they insisted they didn't need a working bathroom or kitchen; they just needed a place to sleep. At this point, we were in the hole almost $8,000, so we said okay.

Well, within thirty minutes of dropping off the trailer at their in-laws' house, I got a frantic call from the guy telling me the power wasn't working. I drove back, and it turned out that instead of hooking up to a generator like you're supposed to, the guy had run about two hundred feet of extension cords from the trailer to a wall outlet in the garage and tripped the breaker. Not only that, but he had also run a garden hose into the trailer so they could brush their teeth, and they almost flooded the floor. Thank goodness the power *wasn't* working!

S: God bless Dan, he ran into town and bought a generator for $700 only to find out the guy's in-laws already had two generators in their basement—they just didn't feel like wheeling them across the yard to the camper.

D: The worst part was, because we didn't have the water hooked up yet, we had given them a massive discount on the rental, so we ended up losing money on the deal.

S: Once we got the water line fixed, we ended up renting out our little farmhouse on wheels so often that we only got to use it once ourselves the entire summer.

D: Sam was right—going the Airbnb route really was a great revenue stream.

S: It was also a great creative outlet. I had gotten so many ideas from looking online at what others had done that I decided to document our entire renovation on Instagram. In addition to the before-and-after photos, Dan and I did a couple of tutorial videos and time-lapse clips showing our progress. In turn, people started sharing their own renovation stories, giving us decorating tips, letting us know where we could find building materials on sale, encouraging us, and even praying for us! It was like I'd found my own little community. More importantly, working on the trailer and posting about it online gave me something fun and exciting to look forward to every day, which helped break me out of my postpartum funk. That alone was worth the $7,000 investment!

D: Eight thousand, babe. Plus another $700 for the generator.

S: Whatever.

The High Cost of Not Living

D: You can't put a price tag on happiness. I knew Sam was having a hard time being at home with the kids by herself all day. What I didn't realize until we started working on the trailer was how much I'd been struggling myself.

At the time, my job was basically assembly-line work, and while I love working with my hands, standing there doing the same repetitive motion day after day was really starting to wear on me. I kept finding myself wondering, *Is this it? Is this really what life is supposed to look like?*

S: I honestly thought it was. I figured, *Okay, you get married, he goes to his job every day, I go to mine, we come home, have dinner, go to bed, wake up, and do it all over again. Add a couple of kids, rinse, and repeat. That's life.*

It's not that I didn't love being a mom, because I did! But Dan and I are both extroverts. We're always on the go, constantly jumping from one thing to another, so to suddenly find ourselves stuck in the same routine for months on end was just—

D: Soul sucking.

S: It was also hard living so far away from our family and friends. I missed going shopping with my sister and being able to call up a group of friends for an impromptu lunch or girls' night. But mostly I missed Dan. He was working forty hours a week, plus overtime, and without my mom to take the kids for us every Friday for our date night, we rarely got to spend any time alone together, and I hated that.

D: So did I. I also hated not getting to spend more time with our kids. My dad was a long-haul trucker, so he was on the road a lot when I was growing up—sometimes five to six days a week. He did his best to make up for it when he was home, but I would've given anything to have had him around more.

S: It was the same with me and my mom. She had to work so much to provide for my sister and me that we didn't get to spend anywhere near as much time together as we would have liked. That's why she put so much energy into planning our road trips. It was her way of making up for lost time.

D: It's funny, a lot of people think that providing for their kids means buying them things, but when I think back on my childhood, I honestly can't remember a single toy. What I remember with crystal clarity are the times my dad took me with him on hunting trips. Even before I was old enough to get a hunting license, he would let me sit next to him out in the woods and watch for deer. We would just sit there side by side for hours, and I loved it. Every once in a while, when he got a few days off in a row, he would take my brother and me up to a remote cabin in Canada to go fishing. And I mean *remote*—we're talking miles from anywhere, with no electricity and no running water. If you had to go, it was either the woods or the *stankiest* outhouse north of the Dakotas. Believe me, there was nothing fancy or high tech about that place, but I didn't care. I just loved spending time alone with my dad. My only regret was that there wasn't enough of it.

S: When we got married, we promised each other we wouldn't let our kids get in the way of enjoying life to the fullest. It never even occurred to us that life might get in the way of us being able to truly enjoy our kids—or each other, for that matter. But that's exactly what was happening.

D: The whole point of moving to Colorado was to have fun and go on adventures together as a family. But since we'd moved there, it felt like all my time and energy were being spent not on the people I loved and the things I loved doing but on a job I really wasn't passionate about and worrying about how we could make ends meet.

S: Even when Dan got time off, everything was so expensive we couldn't afford to go anywhere or do anything anyway. We might as well have been living in Kansas.

D: Brian Dyson, the former CEO of Coca-Cola made a great analogy. He said, "Imagine . . . you are juggling some five balls in the air. You name them work, family, health, friends and spirit. . . . Work is a rubber ball. If you drop it, it will bounce back. But the other four balls . . . are made of glass. If you drop one of these, they will be irrevocably scuffed, marked, nicked, damaged, or even shattered."

He's spot-on—there will always be more work to do. But the time you get to spend with your spouse and your kids is finite: once it's gone, it's gone. Sam and I both had our share of scuff marks from not getting to spend as much time with our parents as we would have liked, and we wanted the narrative to be different for our kids—and for us.

I didn't want to be a "weekend dad," frantically trying to cram a week's worth of activities into two days only to disappear for the next five. I wanted to be an integral part of Canyon and Ember's lives every single day. Our kids hadn't even started school yet, but I could already see where my current momentum was taking me, and I didn't like it. Being able to provide for my family was important, but not if it came at the expense of us actually being a family and spending time with one another.

S: Working on the RV together was like a wake-up call to the kind of life we wanted to live. It was fun. Every day presented a different challenge and an opportunity to try something new.

D: We didn't always know what we were doing, but we had a blast figuring it out, and we loved the sense of accomplishment we got from making something with our own hands.

S: Plus, we were our own bosses.

D: We set our own budgets—

IDEAS TO MAKE THE WORKDAY MORE FUN

- Play innocent pranks (for example, fill someone's office with balloons or cover someone's cubicle with sticky notes).
- Have a cooking contest at lunch.
- Host a potluck.
- Plan a game tournament (for example, fantasy football, March Madness, or board games).
- Create a competition for daily tasks.
- Take a walk at lunch.
- Have a book group or a TV show–watching party.

S: And blew right past them.

D: We set our own deadlines—

S: And blew right past them.

D: We decided when and how long we would work and when we would take a night or a weekend off.

S: Plus, the kids were right there with us the entire time.

D: Best of all, we got to reap the benefits of our own labors. I liked my boss—he was a great guy. But it was frustrating knowing that the work I was doing wasn't really benefiting me in the long run—*and* it was taking me away from my family. It just wasn't worth it. So not long after we finished the trailer, I handed in my two-weeks' notice.

Don't Chase!

D & S: We know what you're thinking: *That's great for you, but I can't just quit my job.* But you know what? You don't have to. One of the most important things we learned during this season was that *choosing* adventure and *chasing* adventure are two different things.

We moved to Colorado because we thought that if we lived near the mountains, we could go skiing, camping, and hunting whenever we wanted to. To us, Colorado *was* adventure—we just had to get there. But once we did, we learned a very valuable—and very expensive—lesson: it doesn't matter *where* you live; it matters *how* you live.

We lived right at the foot of the Rockies for two years and never really got a chance to enjoy them. But when we were living in that little farmhouse outside of Springfield, we had the time of our lives. In fact, we've had far more fun in Missouri than we ever had in Colorado.

D: A few summers ago, Sam and I were out for a walk, and we stumbled across a foot trail that ran down to a creek not far from our apartment. Because it was within walking distance, we decided to take the kids there one afternoon for a picnic. We brought a couple of lounge chairs and sat in the shade with our shoes off and our feet in the water while the kids splashed around in the creek and floated an old plastic Frisbee back and forth to each other.

S: We had so much fun that we ended up going back almost every weekend that summer. One weekend we invited some friends to go with us, and before we knew it, people were calling us up three or four times a month asking, "When are we going to the creek again?"

D: When you talk about having an adventure, most people don't think about standing around in ankle-deep water less than a mile from their house, but we had a blast—and there wasn't a mountain in sight. That's because adventure isn't a state; it's a state of mind.

The same principle applies to work. It's not about quitting your job or getting a different one. It's often about finding ways to bring more fun and excitement to the job you already have.

Making the Nine-to-Five Work

D: Take it from a guy who worked on an assembly line for a while . . . working a nine-to-five job doesn't have to be drudgery. There are a lot of things you can do to add variety to your day and make the time go by a little faster.

When I was working in Colorado, I used to go out for lunch a lot. One day I was talking with a couple of coworkers about which restaurant had the best burritos in town. As it turned out, we all had strong opinions about this, so to make things interesting, a bunch of us decided that twice a week we would go to a different burrito spot together and compare them. We even created a rating sheet to ensure that all of the burritos were being judged on the same criteria, and people *really* got into it (some people also gave wildly biased reviews, which skewed the final results, but that's a rant for another day).

It started with just a handful of us, but before we knew it, almost half the company was participating. In fact, everyone had such a good time that we ended up doing the same thing for breakfast burritos. (Before you ask, yes, there *is* a difference.) This idea wasn't anything big or elaborate, but it got us out of the lunchtime rut, introduced us to a ton of new restaurants we otherwise might not have tried, and gave us a chance to spend time with some people we wouldn't typically interact with. Most importantly, it gave us something fun and different to look forward to every week.

Along these same lines, I once worked in a warehouse where one of the employees brought in an old Ping-Pong table and hosted tournaments once a month. Another place I worked at used to host summer and winter Olympics. We had adult Big Wheel races and played indoor hockey with pool noodles. We had gross food-eating competitions, chili cook-offs, and wing-eating contests. It was awesome, and people genuinely looked forward to it every year.

On a smaller scale, when I was working on the assembly line, one of the other guys and I used to compete to see who could put more units together in ten minutes or an hour. And when things were slow, we put up one of those little suction cup basketball hoops, shot baskets, and played H-O-R-S-E. When that got old, we brought in a football, drew a set of goalposts on the back wall, and competed to kick the longest field goal.

The point is, work can be as dull or as exciting as you make it. You just have to find a way to introduce something you genuinely enjoy into your workday. Start a book club. Bring in your favorite board games to play over lunch. Gather a small group in an empty conference room and do a craft hour or watch an episode of your favorite TV show. Take turns bringing in your favorite cookies or—in my

case—wings. Build in little breaks and give yourself rewards for accomplishing things on your to-do list. Even if it's just treating yourself to something from the vending machine or taking a quick walk around the building every time you answer ten emails, give yourself something to look forward to every day.

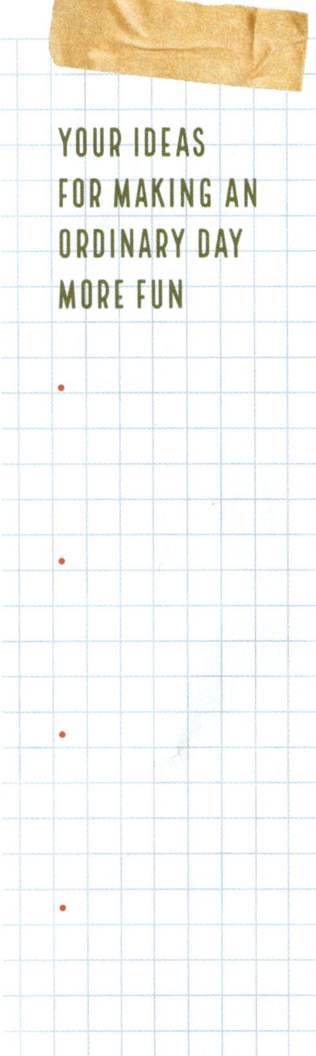

S: In the long-term, take full advantage of your paid time off, and plan regular vacations. Whether it's a week on the coast, a day at the beach, or an afternoon hiking in a local forest preserve, be intentional about building adventure into your schedule—and make it stick! Establish firm boundaries to ensure that your work time doesn't bleed into your "you time," and keep your nights and weekends free to spend with your family and do something you want to do. Because if you don't make adventure a priority, it will get lost in the shuffle.

D: As bestselling author Stephen Covey wrote, "The key is not to prioritize what's on your schedule, but to schedule your priorities." I love to hunt, so one of my nonnegotiables is having the flexibility to take several long weekends off during deer season every fall. If a job can't or won't allow for that, I simply won't take the job.

S: For me, the nonnegotiable is having quality time with the kids. Right after I had Canyon, I got a job working as an assistant for the youth group at our church. They let me bring him with me a few days a week, and he would nap while I worked on the computer, ran copies, and answered the phone, but it wasn't what I would call quality time. At the time, I also had a side gig coordinating weddings, and one day it occurred to me that I could coordinate one wedding a month and make as much money in one weekend as I could in four weeks at the church—and have worlds more time to spend with Canyon. So as much as I genuinely enjoyed working at the church and loved the people, I decided to quit.

The extra money would have been nice, but it wasn't worth the connection time I was missing out on with my son.

Again, we get that quitting your job might not be an option. We're just saying don't get so busy making a living that you forget to make a *life*.

D: For us, living in Colorado had become unmanageable—financially, relationally, and emotionally. We missed having friends and family nearby, and I wanted to find a way to make a living that was not only meaningful for me but also gave me a chance to spend more time with Sam and the kids.

I didn't know exactly what I was going to do, but now that I had a sense of how profitable it could be to rent out the trailer, I started toying with the idea of buying more of them and outfitting them as hunting campers that we could rent out during deer season. And you know where there are plenty of deer? Back home in Missouri. With no money and no place to live, Sam was about to get her wish. We were going to be moving into the trailer full-time.

That meant we had some serious downsizing to do.

SOMETIMES

YOU HAVE TO

Make Your

Own Fun.

7

THE Path Less Traveled

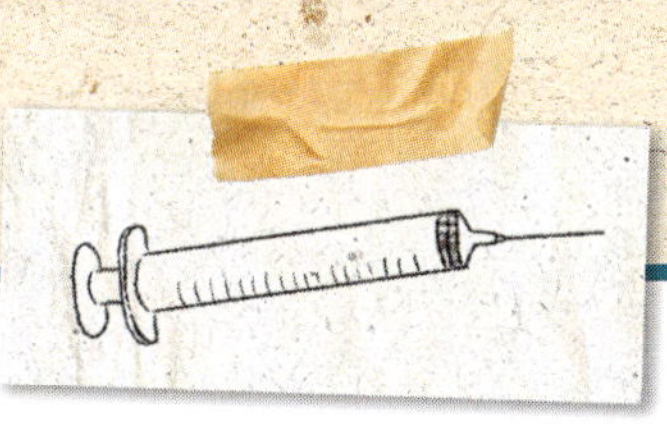

S: A lot of people associate adventure and risk-taking with spontaneity—flying to Las Vegas to get married, stopping by a dealership "just to take a look" and driving away in a brand-new SUV—

D: That time I wanted to meet Brett Favre.

S: Oh, yeah . . . that was classic Dan. We were at a fundraiser, and they were raffling off these high-end items. One of them was a three-day deer hunt with Brett Favre. Needless to say, as a massive Packers fan and a hunter, Dan almost lost his ever-loving mind. The next thing I knew, he was looking at me wild-eyed, going, "Babe, can we sell the car?" We didn't, by the way.

D: And I've always regretted it.

S: Yeah . . . I haven't. But while we have made our fair share of spontaneous decisions over the years—like the time we drove thirteen hours to go to the wedding

of a couple we'd just met online or when we signed a twelve-month lease on an apartment, sight unseen—without question, the riskiest thing we've ever done was actually the least spontaneous, and it all started with a little math.

1 + 1 = Done

S: Dan has four siblings. I have one, but growing up, I always wished I had more. So when we first got married, we decided we would split the difference and have four kids.

D: I wanted to have all our kids by the time I was thirty-two. That way the youngest one would be eighteen and out of the house by the time I hit fifty.

S: We did the math and realized that if we got pregnant as soon as each baby hit nine months, we could have all four by the time Dan was thirty-two. So after sailing through my first pregnancy—during which I was able to keep running all the way up through my thirty-eighth week—and then giving birth to the most laid-back baby in the world, I was like, *Dang, that was awesome! Let's do this again!*

D: Then we had Ember. Her name basically means "a little spark of fire that never burns out," and man, does it fit her. From the moment we brought her home from the hospital, she brought light and warmth to our lives, just like her namesake. But she also kinda set our expectations on fire. The tiniest sound would wake her up, and when she got fussy, there was almost nothing you could do to console her.

S: Dan and I would just look at each other like, *What are we doing wrong?*

D: They responded to things so differently. You could take a pacifier away from Ember for just a second, and she would become hysterical. Meanwhile, you could practically pepper spray Canyon and he'd be like, "Yeah? That's all you got?"

S: Even the postpartum experience was different. With Canyon, I had one day of baby blues and that was it. With Ember, not only were we hundreds of miles away from family and friends, but I also had mastitis. (Don't ask. If you know, you know.) I was in a lot of pain, and that made my postpartum journey a lot harder. So when Ember hit nine months, I looked at Dan and said, "What do you think?"

"I love both of our kids to death," he said. "But here's the thing: what if the next one is an all-out wildfire? I don't know if we have what it takes to go from man-to-man to zone defense."

As much as I hated to admit it, he was right. We were officially at our limit, kid-wise. We had one of each and a 1:1 parent-kid ratio, and for us, that was perfect. There was just one problem: I really missed labor and pregnancy.

D: Um, babe . . . I was there, and I can promise you, you didn't really enjoy labor.

S: Yeah, labor was hard—especially the last fifteen minutes or so. But look what you get at the end of it! It's so unthinkably fascinating to me that our bodies are capable of growing another human being. I loved pregnancy, especially watching how my body miraculously transformed to create a safe place for our babies to grow. And when it came time to deliver, I had Dan, my mom, my sister, and my friend in the room with me, holding my hand, cheering me on, and praying for me the entire time. But because I didn't realize Ember would be our last, I didn't get to fully appreciate that "final" pregnancy. So even though I was 100 percent on board with the decision to stop at two, a big part of me was like, *Dang, I'd love to be pregnant again.*

A Not-So-Modest Proposal

S: Not long after Ember was born, I was talking with a friend who was a mother of three. After catching up on what all our kids were doing, she sat back and casually asked, "So . . . are you guys going to have another one?"

Fresh off the conversation with Dan, I said, "I don't think so. We've got one of each, so we feel like we're good. But . . ." I admitted somewhat hesitantly, "I'd like to be pregnant again. I don't want to parent a third child, which I realize probably sounds awful, but I'd really love to *have* another baby."

She just stared at me for a second, and I readied myself for her comeback. Instead, she leaned forward, smiled, and said, "You know what you should do, Sam? You should be a surrogate."

Surrogate? I knew what the term meant, but aside from seeing the Tina Fey and Amy Poehler movie *Baby Mama* (which, by the way, isn't the best depiction of what surrogacy actually looks like), I didn't know much about it. That afternoon, I went home and started doing a little research.

I started with the basics: What is surrogacy? From there, I moved on to the difference between traditional surrogacy and gestational surrogacy. (In case you're wondering, traditional surrogacy is when the surrogate's eggs are used, so she is biologically related to the baby she is carrying. In gestational surrogacy, the surrogate has no biological link to the baby whatsoever. She just provides the womb.) Then I looked at what would be required of me as a surrogate. It was quite a list and included everything from having had at least one previous successful pregnancy with no complications, a clean bill of health, and a BMI of 30 or lower, to financial stability, a good support system, and the ability to travel. On the upside, I seemed to match all the required criteria to a tee.

What I *wasn't* sure about—and what wasn't covered in any of the lists—was how it would feel to give up a baby that I'd carried for nine months. I wondered if I'd even be able to do it.

After poking around online a little longer, I stumbled across a documentary on YouTube that focused on what they called "transition postpartum," which is the emotional impact of handing the newborn baby over to the intended parents. The video was surprisingly helpful. They talked about how knowing that it's not your

HAVING KIDS TEACHES YOU SO MUCH ABOUT YOURSELF—MOST IMPORTANTLY, IT HELPS YOU REALIZE HOW GOD SEES YOU.

child from the very beginning resets your brain. You're not planning a nursery. You're not picking out a name. You're not buying outfits. So while you're still emotionally invested in the journey, thinking about the baby and praying for the baby, your feelings aren't necessarily "maternal." Of course, saying it was one thing; actually *doing* it would be another.

But the more testimonials I read by parents talking about meeting their biological babies for the first time—many of whom had been through years of infertility and had suffered multiple miscarriages—I just couldn't let go of the idea. I wondered what it would be like to make that moment and all the moments after that possible for couples who longed to be parents.

A few days later, Dan and I were driving home from the store, and I casually threw out, "Babe, you know how I've talked about how much I miss pregnancy and delivery and labor?" He got this panicked look on his face.

D: I thought for sure she was going to tell me she was pregnant.

Then she hit me with . . . "I really feel like I should have a baby for somebody else."

I am not usually at a loss for words. But this time, I was choking on air.

S: When Dan didn't say anything, I tried again. "I want to be a surrogate."

D: Honestly, I wasn't even sure what that meant. Regardless, my first reaction was, "No way. We're not going to give our baby to someone else."

S: "That's just it," I explained. "It wouldn't be *our* baby. It would be another couple's egg and sperm. Genetically, we wouldn't be related to the baby at all. I'd just be carrying the baby for them."

1,000 CALORIE GRANOLA BAR RECIPE[1]

Ingredients

3/4 lb. softened butter

2 cups sugar (I used half brown sugar, half regular sugar)

1/3 cup light corn syrup

1/3 cup honey

1 tsp. maple flavoring (I used vanilla)

3/4 cup ground nuts (I used walnuts)

9 cups one-minute oats

Instructions

Grind up the oats in a blender or food processor.

In a large mixing bowl, cream together all the ingredients except the nuts and oats.

Once it's blended, stir in the oats and nuts. Make sure it's well mixed.

Spread the mixture onto a cookie sheet with at least a ½-inch lip. Press down the mixture and pack it until it fills the pan and is a smidge less than ½-inch thick. (You'll probably need a second sheet.)

Bake at 325 degrees for 15 minutes. Remove and press down with a spatula to prevent crumbling when it cools. (If you bake it too long, it gets hard and crunchy.)

While it's still warm, cut into three-inch squares.

Optional: You can add raisins with the nuts.

---

1 Used with permission from Charles L. Sommers Alumni Association, Inc., https://www.holry.org.

D: There were about thirty-six million questions running through my mind at that point. *Are you kidding me? Where did this come from all of a sudden? Did I miss an earlier conversation? Has someone actually asked you to do this?* But somehow, the one that bubbled to the top was, "You'd be able to do that, you think? Just give the baby up at the end? You wouldn't feel any connection to the baby at all?"

S: "I'm not saying it would be easy, but based on everything I've read, it sounds like it would be 100 percent worth it. I mean, what if we couldn't have kids of our own? Can you imagine our lives without Canyon and Ember?"

D: Honestly, I couldn't.

"It just feels like if I *could* do that for another couple, why wouldn't I?" she said.

I wasn't sure what to think. On the one hand, she seemed genuine. Then again, a couple of months back, when we were watching an episode of *Cops*, a female police officer came on screen, and Sam was like, "Oh my gosh, it would be so much fun to be a police officer!" and she started talking about joining the academy. For all I knew, this could have been the same kind of thing, so I figured, *I'll just humor her, and in a couple of days, she'll forget all about it.*

"Okay, tell you what," I said. "Why don't we pray about it?"

"Deal."

S: What I didn't tell Dan was that I'd already been praying about it—a lot.

D: A few days later, we had a second conversation on the topic. As Sam started walking me though all the research she'd done about finding a surrogacy agency, getting background checks, and taking IVF meds, I thought, *Oh, shoot, this isn't going to go away. This is for real.*

What really convinced me it was something I needed to start taking seriously, though, was when she said, "Honestly, this has nothing to do with me. I mean, no, I didn't expect Ember to be our last baby, and I *have* been struggling with the fact that I don't feel like I'm ready to be finished with pregnancy and labor yet. I love what my body is able to do—to create and grow and nurture and bring new life into the world—and just knowing that there are people out there who can't do that when I not only *can* but *want* to . . . Why not help somebody else have what we have? Yes, it's nine months of my life. And yes, labor is intense, but it just feels like such a minuscule thing for me to go through if it means giving someone else a lifetime of love with a child. I really feel like the Lord put this on my heart and he's calling me to do this."

One of the things I love about Sam is that she has always had a tender, caring heart, and she loves to help others. If we're driving down the road and we see somebody pulled off to the side, she always says, "Let's stop and see if they need help." She's always making care packages of gently used clothes and toys that our kids have outgrown to gift to other young families who are struggling. That's just who she is. Anytime she sees someone in need, she immediately wants to step in. The way I saw it, this was just her way of meeting a bigger need.

And for what it's worth, I totally agreed with her. Being a dad has been one of the greatest experiences of my life. Having kids has taught me much about myself, not the least of which is how God sees me. I've always understood that I have two dads—my earthly dad and my heavenly Father. But now that I have kids, whenever they struggle with something—whether it's wanting a snack out of a cabinet they can't reach, trying to put together a puzzle, working on a math problem for school, or crying over a toy they can't find—and they come to me for help, it reminds me how much God loves us, how he hates to see us struggle, and how much he wants us to come to him for help.

And then there's the sheer delight of watching them discover something new in nature or seeing their joy in doing something they love—like the smile that comes across Ember's face when she draws or paints, or how excited Canyon gets when he builds a cool blanket fort in the living room or shows off his latest karate kicks. There's nothing else like it in the world.

For those reasons alone, as far as I was concerned, if Sam genuinely believed this was a leading from the Lord, and she was willing to put her body through nine months of pregnancy, labor, and delivery to bless someone else the way we had been blessed—I was all in.

S: I want to point out here that I know there are a lot of different (and strong!) opinions about surrogacy. I get that—it's a complex scenario, and it's not for everyone. We don't claim to be experts; we just decided that, for us, this felt like a pro-life act of love that would bless another family.

D: Once we'd decided all lights were green, I just had one question. "So . . . *now* what do we do?"

So . . . You Wanna Have Someone Else's Baby

S: Once Dan was on board, I started reaching out to different surrogacy agencies in the Denver area. The first agency never called me back, and the second was downright rude on the phone. But the third one was super sweet. They sent me an application, I passed along my medical records, and they started their background check. That process alone took several months.

Meanwhile, they had us meet with a psychologist. Dan's part went great, but when she told me I needed to take a three-hundred-question personality test, I panicked. I've never been a good test taker. This brought flashbacks of tests in nursing school (which never panned out for me, by the way).

I was taking a pharmacology class, and on the final exam, there were a bunch of questions about the side effects of specific drugs, like "What stat would indicate that a patient was having a severe reaction to furosemide?" The problem is, a lot of times there was more than one correct answer. For example, a patient might exhibit both an elevated heart rate *and* elevated blood pressure, and while technically both are correct, the *more* definitive stat would be the blood pressure. So even when I was right, I was wrong—or at least, not right enough.

D: It's kind of like how all thumbs are fingers, but not all fingers are thumbs.

S: Not helpful, babe. Anyway, this particular test was a lot like that. There were a ton of "What would you do . . . ?" and "How would you feel . . . ?" questions, and the answers were on a sliding scale of "strongly agree," "agree," "neutral," "disagree," or "strongly disagree."

D: You're just supposed to give your gut response, but Sam kept overthinking everything.

S: Well, it was hard. There would be a statement like "I get extremely angry when somebody breaks the law." Obviously, I don't *like* it when somebody breaks the law, but I wouldn't say it makes me "extremely angry." But if I don't say, "strongly agree," does that make it look like I'm okay with it? Then again, if I say, "strongly agree," does that sound like I'm overly judgmental or I have anger issues? It also depends on what law is being broken. I mean, are we talking jaywalking or homicide here?

D: See the problem?

S: Anyway, I ended up scoring a tick below the agency's minimum requirements, and that really shook me. We'd been praying about this for months by this point, and we both felt peace about it. But if I couldn't even pass the personality test required to work with an agency, how would this ever happen?

D: All we could do was pray: *Lord, if this isn't your will, keep closing the doors. But if it is your will, help us find a way.*

S: A few weeks later, we got together with a couple we'd met through Instagram, and in the course of the conversation, we found out that her sister was a surrogate. I know! What are the odds, right? Anyway, when I asked her which agency her sister went through, she told me she didn't use one. She met her intended parents on Facebook.

D: We were like, "Hold up. *Facebook*?"

S: It turns out, there are a whole bunch of surrogacy match groups on Facebook. It basically works like a dating profile. You put up your information, upload a few pictures, and wait to see if you get a match.

D: And before you say, "That sounds a little shady," at its core, a surrogacy agency essentially serves as a matchmaker at first, helping you find compatible couples, and then as a middleman between the intended parents, the surrogate parents, and the fertility clinic, scheduling appointments, shuffling paperwork, and sending payments back and forth. And while these agencies are extremely helpful—especially when you're going through this for the first time—they're not the *only* way.

As we discovered firsthand, the legal side of surrogacy can be extremely complicated, so whether you go through an agency or take the independent route, lawyers are brought in and consulted before anything remotely medical takes place. Everything is intentionally thought through and meticulously planned and documented. I mean, we're talking about a human life.

S: To that end, before we even reached out to our first agency, Dan and I discussed the potential pitfalls of surrogacy at length and decided that we had three nonnegotiables. First, unless there was a serious threat to my life, terminating the pregnancy would be off the table. Second, we wanted a husband-and-wife couple. Third, we wanted this to be an open relationship. By that, we mean we wanted to stay in contact with the intended parents after the baby was born. We didn't want this match to be strictly transactional, where we handed the baby over and that was it. After all, surrogacy is an incredibly personal process. Whoever we got matched with would be coming along to my appointments and checkups, they'd be privy to all my medical information, and they would be present at the birth. Plus, Dan and I were going to be physically, emotionally, and spiritually invested in this journey for the better part of a year, if not longer, and we wanted to be able to celebrate that baby's life for years to come.

D: We weren't asking to be invited to every birthday party, holiday gathering, and family event. We understand how emotional this process can be for the intended couple. But given our own level of involvement and risk, we wanted to at least be able to send the occasional gift or card, get updates about milestones, and be treated as friends of the family.

S: Also, while it wasn't a complete nonnegotiable, we were hoping to find a couple who would be open to sharing the journey online. In all my research, I hadn't been able to find anyone on social media who had documented the entire journey from start to finish—what the matching process was like, how the appointments worked, or how to navigate the delicate balance of sharing and celebrating every twinge, kick, and milestone with a mother who is grieving not being able to experience it firsthand. I would have given anything for that.

D: We weren't asking them to document anything, but we were hoping to get their blessing for us to share our side of the journey.

WHETHER OR NOT THE STARS ALIGN,
WE CAN TRUST THAT WHATEVER HAPPENS,
GOD IS STILL GOOD.

S: We could still do that without sharing who the intended couple was, and we wanted to be able to encourage and educate others who might feel called to either become or engage a surrogate.

D: By the way, back when we were first talking with an agency, they informed us that our list of criteria might make it difficult for us to find a compatible match—especially because of the no-termination clause.

S: We understand—surrogacy isn't cheap. They would be covering all the appointments, plus medical, travel, and incidental expenses, not to mention fertility treatments, embryo transfer, and hospital stays, so from start to finish, the whole process can easily run upwards of $75,000 to $100,000. When you put that much money into something, of course you want a healthy baby at the end. From a financial perspective, we could appreciate that. But from a spiritual perspective, Dan and I believe *all* babies are a blessing and worthy of life. That's something we feel very strongly about, and if that meant we had to wait six months, a year, or even longer to find a compatible match, we were okay with that.

D: One hundred percent.

S: So after I spent a few days reading other people's posts and seeing how it was done, I went ahead and posted my own profile.

> Hey, everyone. My name is Sam! I have been married to my husband for almost eight years. We have two kids, and we would love to help another couple start/add to their family!! This will be my first time being a surrogate, but it's something my husband and I have talked about, researched, and prayed about for a while now! We have our families' support.
>
> A little about me:
>
> - 28 years old
> - I live in southern Missouri. Willing to travel!
> - Drug-/smoke-/alcohol-free living

- I had two easy pregnancies and natural full-term births (we are done having kids).
- BMI: 21
- I live an active lifestyle. As a family we enjoy hiking, camping, reno/design, and traveling!
- Desire husband and wife IPs [intended parents]
- Against termination unless my life is at risk
- Would love to stay in touch after birth! I desire a close relationship with our IPs.
- Willing to share all pictures, travel for visits, and be very open throughout the whole pregnancy and labor!
- Willing to pump post birth.
- Open to doing independent or through an agency if you've already started the process with one.

Then I uploaded some pics of me, Dan, and the kids, and within a few days, we had ten different couples reach out to us. There were a couple of false starts, like the first couple we matched with. They were incredibly sweet and had been trying for years to have a baby. So we went through the whole screening process, signed all the paperwork, and got started on the fertility treatment prep, but for some reason my uterine lining wasn't thickening the way we hoped. While we were trying to resolve that, they ended up getting pregnant naturally!

D: That was wild.

S: Totally. We couldn't have been happier for them. Still, it was hard for us—especially me. I was starting to think maybe it wasn't meant to happen after all. But I genuinely believed the Lord was calling me to do this, so we kept trying.

HAVING FAITH HELPS US REMEMBER THAT THE WEIGHT ISN'T ALL ON OUR SHOULDERS.

D: By the way, I love how you forgot to mention my name in that Facebook write-up.

S: Oh my gosh, I am so sorry, babe. Actually, I'm glad you called that out, because I cannot emphasize enough how important Dan's role was throughout this process. I always tell people who are considering surrogacy—or any significant life change, for that matter—to make sure your spouse is 100 percent on board before you commit, because it will impact both of you. Yes, I was the one actually carrying the baby, but Dan supported me mentally, emotionally, spiritually, and physically. Plus, there were stretches when I was so tired I had to take two, sometimes three naps a day, during which Dan was acting as Mom *and* Dad—picking up the kids from school, helping them with their homework, cleaning the apartment, doing the laundry, making dinner, and running through the drive-thru to feed my sudden Taco Bell cravings.

D: And the shots. Don't forget about the shots.

S: That's right! Once we found a match, I had to have several months' worth of progesterone shots to get my body ready to accept the embryo. There was *no way* I was going to be able to do those myself, so poor Dan had to learn.

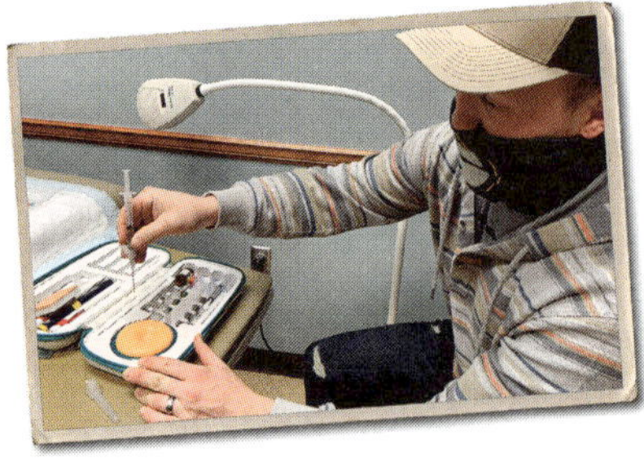

D: Bear in mind, I had never given anyone a shot in my life. Then at Sam's first appointment, the nurse looked at me and said, "Okay, so I'm assuming you're going to be administering the shots, right?"

S: The color literally drained from Dan's face, and he kind of stammered, "Yeah . . . I guess so."

D: So anyway, she held up a needle and a little vial of liquid and said, "You just draw up one milliliter of progesterone, and make sure there aren't any air bubbles in it . . ." As she's talking, I'm thinking, *Wait. How do I know if there are any air bubbles in it? And what if there are? What if I accidentally give Sam an embolism?*

Meanwhile, the nurse had now taken a permanent marker and drawn a tiny square on Sam's butt cheek. Then she turned to me and said, "You're going to want to inject it in or around this area." I was thinking, *You gotta be kidding me. This is way too much.* Then she handed me the needle, reached into her coat pocket, and pulled out a little flesh-colored puck that looked like one of those "Easy" buttons from the old Staples commercials. She said, "Now, you want to do it quickly, because if you go too slowly, it's going to be very painful for your wife."

I looked at Sam, who was still leaning over the edge of the table with her yoga pants halfway down. She gave me this nervous glance, like, *Please don't screw this up.* Practically with my eyes closed, I jabbed the needle into the little puck and squeezed the plunger.

"Perfect!" she said.

And I was like, *Was it?* I mean, the needle was still stuck in the puck, which, based on her expression, didn't do a lot for Sam's confidence level. The next thing I knew, the nurse was handing me a box full of vials, syringes, gauze pads, alcohol swabs, and bandages, and I was feeling about two seconds away from an embolism myself. I mean, people go to school for like eight years to learn how to do this properly, and this woman just showed me how to do it in thirteen seconds. And I had to do it seventy times! Seventy!

S: Well, it wasn't exactly a picnic for me either . . .

D: Of course, there *was* an upside. Once Sam started showing, people came up to me beaming, saying, "Congratulations!" And you should have seen the looks on their faces when I said, "Thanks, but the baby's not mine." Then they'd look at Sam, horrified, and she'd say, "It's not mine either." I'm telling you, it almost made those seventy shots worth it.

TEN WAYS TO PAY IT FORWARD

1. Surprise a friend with dinner.
2. Anonymously leave flowers on someone's windshield.
3. Leave encouraging notes in books borrowed from the library.
4. Pay for someone in the drive-thru.
5. Clean the house for a mom with a newborn.
6. Fill up a stranger's gas tank.
7. Offer to babysit so a couple you know can go on a date night.
8. Offer snacks and drinks to delivery carriers.
9. Give gift cards to teachers, bus drivers, and crossing guards.
10. Bring food to your local fire station.

S: But to be there the moment a new life enters the world and see the look of pure joy on the parents' faces as they hold *their* baby for the first time? I'd happily suffer through seven hundred shots for that.

Worth the Risk

S: There's no question, the surrogacy journey has been the most physically, emotionally, and spiritually challenging adventure we've ever undertaken. It has also been the most rewarding.

But it wasn't something we entered into lightly, because this time it wasn't just about us. We could buy an old school bus and rip out the insides, drive cross-country to do a reality show, or up and move to Colorado on a dime (almost literally), and if it didn't work out, we might be out a few thousand bucks and have to tighten our belts a little until we bounced back. But with the surrogacy journey, there was literally a life in the balance—three of them, in fact: the intended parents and their baby.

D: This isn't something I like to spend a lot of time thinking about, but Sam's life was at risk as well. Even though we'd already had two kids of our own, we had no idea how her body would react to the shots, the embryo transfer, or a foreign pregnancy. Thank God, nothing bad happened. But when it's a question of life and death, or when the health and welfare of other people are involved, it's wise not to just rush headlong into it. Everything has to be weighed out and thought through very carefully.

S: Even if we hadn't spent countless hours in prayer and conversation prior to starting our journey (which we did), the whole process is designed to make you slow down and

THERE'S UNEXPECTED JOY THAT COMES FROM SETTING YOUR OWN COMFORT AND CONVENIENCE ASIDE FOR THE SAKE OF SOMEONE ELSE.

think through everything more carefully. During our initial screening process, our surrogacy psychologist asked us tons of questions about our marriage, our support system, how our families felt about all this, if we'd thought through the potential health risks and the physical and emotional strain, if we were prepared to deal with the possibility of a miscarriage, how we planned to prepare our kids for the fact that the baby would not be coming home with us, how we felt about having another couple speak into my diet, daily activities, and travel plans—it was a lot. But it was important. We needed to be mentally prepared—to be sure we'd thought through everything and this wasn't something we decided to do on a whim.

But once we committed to doing this, the journey became priority one, and everything else fell into place. And make no mistake, it was a journey. It took almost three years from the time I started thinking about surrogacy to our first transfer with our IPs. Three years of waiting, praying, hoping, worrying, testing, and filling out paperwork, not to mention meeting with doctors, counselors, and lawyers—and that was before I even got pregnant!

D: The fact that Sam never wavered in her desire to do this is—to me, anyway—proof that it was the Lord's leading. I mean, we tend to jump from one thing to another at the drop of a hat. *Let's go here! Let's try this! Let's buy that!* And then after a couple of days or weeks, we're on to something else. But when it came to helping another couple start a family, Sam was laser focused.

Psalm 37:5 says, "Commit everything you do to the Lord. Trust him, and he will help you"—and that's exactly what Sam did. Not only did God bless another couple with a family as a result of her obedience and commitment, but that journey gave birth to some pretty significant—and awesome—changes in our lives as well.

S: We'll talk more about that in a minute. But before we move on, please hear me say this: nobody was more surprised than I was when God first placed surrogacy on my heart in 2018.

D: I don't know, babe. I was pretty thrown by it.

S: Correction: nobody was more surprised than we were when the Lord first placed surrogacy on my heart in 2018. And while the journey was hard and painful at times, it was also 100 percent worth it.

For one thing, it gave me a whole new appreciation for Dan. There were so many moments when I felt physically and emotionally weak. But Dan was always there, encouraging me, lifting me up, praying both with me and for me, and reminding me that I was strong and that I was capable of doing hard things.

He also had to deal with the occasional backlash from people who didn't understand what gestational surrogacy was or why we were doing it. And he shouldered more than his fair share of, "Dude, you let somebody else get your wife pregnant?" comments. But to Dan's credit, he took every subtle (and some not-so-subtle) jab in stride and treated each confrontation as an opportunity not only to educate others but also to share his faith.

Speaking of which, this experience also grew our relationship with the Lord. Every time I wasn't feeling well, my numbers weren't where they needed to be, or the couples we thought we were compatible with ended up not being "the ones," the two of us would come together in prayer. And I'm telling you, we leaned *hard* into God and his Word during this journey, especially this promise he made to Jeremiah: "'For I know the plans I have for you,' declares the Lord, 'plans to prosper you and not to harm you, plans to give you hope and a future'" (Jeremiah 29:11).

So many stars have to align for a surrogacy journey to work, both relationally and medically. Whether or not those stars aligned, we had to trust that whatever happened, God was still good.

Even if the surrogacy agencies rejected us, God was still good.

Even if our first few matches didn't work out, God was still good.

Even if the embryo transfer didn't take, God was still good.

Even if I was so nauseous I couldn't take my kids to school, God was still good.

And yes, even if I miscarried, God would still be good.

Having that faith to hold on to throughout the journey was incredibly comforting, because it helped me remember that the weight wasn't all on my shoulders and that even if the surrogacy wasn't successful, God was still in control. He still had a plan, and whatever it was, it was good.

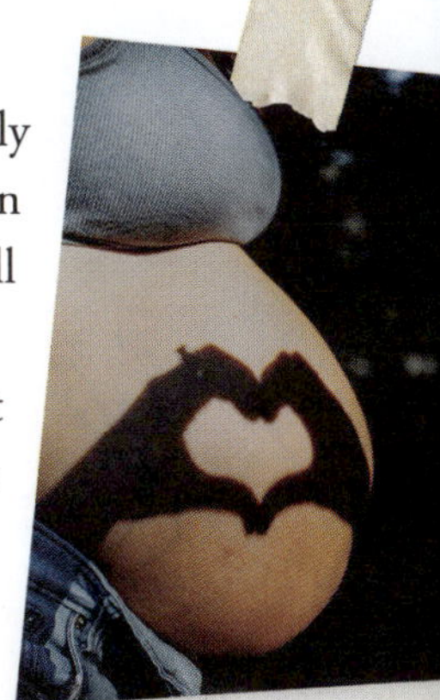

This experience also taught me humility and the unexpected joy that comes from setting your own comfort and convenience aside for the sake of someone else. It's human nature, I think, to hyperfocus on ourselves—what *we* want and how *we* want to be treated—but the truth is, it's so much more fulfilling to serve others. I must have heard "It is more blessed to give than to receive" a thousand times growing up, but I don't know that I ever fully appreciated what it meant until I became a surrogate. I was utterly and completely overwhelmed by love the first time I held Canyon and Ember, and yet I can't even find the words to describe the feeling I got watching our IPs hold their baby for the first time. It truly was a holy experience.

So the next time you feel as though the Lord is leading you to do something—even if, at first blush, it sounds completely nonsensical to you, your spouse, your family, or your friends—don't be afraid to pursue it. Maybe it's renovating an RV or having a baby for someone else or something completely different. If God continues to confirm this path for you and open doors, keep walking through them, no matter how long it takes. You might be surprised by how much the journey itself teaches, shapes, and grows you as a person. In my case, I literally *did* grow a person. But in the process, I also learned more about myself, my marriage, and my faith than I had ever dreamed possible.

D: And RVs, babe. Don't forget we learned a lot about RVs.

S: Oh yeah . . . we definitely learned a lot about RVs.

WHEN GOD PLACES SOMETHING

ON YOUR HEART—

No Matter

How Outrageous

IT MIGHT SEEM TO OTHERS—

Prayerfully

Follow Through.

8

LEAVING IT *All Behind*

D: There's a great scene in Mel Brooks's classic *Star Wars* spoof, *Spaceballs*, that sums up Sam's approach to "downsizing" perfectly. When their space Winnebago runs out of gas while rescuing Princess Vespa, Captain Lone Starr and his faithful half-man, half-dog sidekick, Barf, have to make an emergency landing on a small moon, where they have to travel on foot to the nearest outpost for help. Having no idea how far they'll have to walk, Lone Starr tells the princess, "Take only what you need to survive."

In the next scene, Lone Starr, Barf, Princess Vespa, and her droid, Dot Matrix, are all staggering across a vast desert—the princess carrying nothing, Dot holding a parasol over the princess's head with one hand and pulling three pieces of matching floral luggage behind her in the other, and Lone Starr and Barf (who has a large floral-patterned garment bag draped across his back) several yards behind them, each lugging one end of a giant floral-patterned steamer trunk.

Exhausted, Lone Starr stops and tells Barf to put the trunk down. He then opens the trunk and pulls out the only item in it—an enormous blow dryer—and asks in exasperation, "What's this? I said take only what you need to survive." The princess fires back, "It's my industrial-strength hair dryer—and I *can't* live without it!"

S: Soooo . . . where are you going with this, babe?

D: Once it was decided that we would be moving into the trailer, we agreed that we were going to get rid of everything in our apartment that wasn't 100 percent necessary.

S: Hey, I got rid of a ton of stuff! We sold the dining room table and chairs, our bed, the love seat, the recliner, the coffee table . . . Plus, we got rid of most of the kids' toys, that old playpen we never used, the extra crib . . . And whatever we couldn't sell, we pitched, donated to Goodwill, or left next to the dumpster with a sign that said, "Free! Be blessed."

D: Uh-huh. So, as I was carrying a pair of old floor lamps to the dumpster, I turned around, and there was Sam, lugging these big, clunky barstools to the trailer. I said, "Um, we're moving into a twenty-two-foot trailer. We don't need four barstools."

S: Come on, there was *no way* I was leaving those behind.

D: They were totally unnecessary.

S: But they were a great deal! I found them on Facebook Marketplace. They had black wrought-iron frames and cherry-stained seats, and there were four of them for only $100!

D: What Sam failed to mention is that our tiny dungeon of an apartment had neither a bar nor a counter high enough to accommodate said barstools.

S: Yeah, but they were *really* nice. New, they would have easily cost four or five hundred dollars.

D: Yeah, but . . . never mind. Just tell the story.

S: I wasn't a huge fan of the cherry finish, and since Dan had a sander at work, I asked him to sand the seats down to the original wood.

D: It was a nightmare. They had at least three coats of stain, plus a thick polyurethane coat on top. I went through sanding pad after sanding pad after sanding pad.

S: It ended up taking him several weeks to get them done.

D: Fortunately, since we had no actual use for them, there was no rush.

S: But they looked so much better! A little over a year later, we moved out of the windowless dungeon into a slightly bigger apartment that had a high kitchen counter, so we were finally able to use them!

D: Yeah, for like ten months. But now we were moving into a tiny camper with very limited counter space.

S: But you worked so hard on those! And where are we ever going to find a deal like that again?

D: In fairness, one of the things I love about Sam is her ability to sniff out a bargain. A few years ago, she bought two admittedly beautiful acacia wood poolside lounge chairs on Facebook Marketplace—still in the original packaging. They retailed for $350 apiece, and she got them for just $70 each.

S: That was an *awesome* deal!

D: Agreed. Granted, it would have been an even better deal if we'd actually had a pool.

S: It was an act of faith, babe. I knew one day we'd have a house with a pool.

D: The point is, even though we had neither the room nor the need for four barstools, Sam refused to leave them behind. So we ended up dragging them back with us to Missouri, where they sat in Sam's grandparents' garage for four—count 'em—*four* years, until we finally got an apartment with high countertops.

S: Of course, by then, our decor had completely changed, and they didn't go with anything. But I found an even better set at a discount store for $25 that retailed at Target for $180!

D: And she *still* refused to get rid of or resell the first set. So we now have eight barstools—four that are once again sitting in storage and four new ones—all because Sam flat out refuses to let go of something she got a "great deal" on.

S: I'm sorry. Was I the one who wanted to strap a sixteen-foot canoe to the top of the trailer?

D: Aw, come on, that's apples to oranges, babe.

S: Okay, go ahead and make your case.

D: Shortly after we moved to Colorado, I bought an aluminum canoe on Facebook Marketplace.

S: Which he only used twice.

D: Yeah, but only because I didn't have anyone out in Colorado to go canoeing with. But I had a bunch of friends back in Missouri who loved canoeing, so it would have been a colossal mistake not to bring it back with us.

S: The problem was that the canoe was too big to fit in the trailer.

WE'RE WILLING TO TAKE SO MANY RISKS BECAUSE WE TRUST THAT GOD WILL PROVIDE WHATEVER WE NEED TO GET BY.

D: It fit on top of the trailer, but without any roof rails, there was no way to strap it down. And since our Denali had been stolen while we were in Alaska, all we had left was Sam's Toyota Camry. There was no way we were going to be able to drive 750 miles with a sixteen-foot canoe strapped to the roof. So just as I was about to admit defeat and post it on Facebook Marketplace, my buddy Drew from back home called.

It turned out he was in Colorado picking up a classic car for his brother's lot, and when I told him about the canoe, he said, "Don't you dare sell it! We would have a blast with that thing! I have my pickup with me—just bring it to Denver, and I'll drive it back for you."

I thought, *Sweet!* I grabbed some ratchet straps and tied it to the top of Sam's Camry.

S: It looked ridiculous. The ends of the canoe hung all the way down over both bumpers. And since my Camry didn't have roof rails either, Dan just looped the straps over the top of the canoe and through the doors. One good updraft, and the whole car would have been airborne.

D: It would have been totally worth it though.

S: For a $200 canoe?

D: Come on, it came with a trolling motor, two oars, and four life jackets.

S: Which, by the way, we also brought with us, because, you know . . . downsizing.

D: Anyway, I made it to Denver, Drew and I got the canoe strapped onto his pickup, and he headed out. A few hours later, Sam and I were getting ready to leave ourselves, and Drew called me from a rest stop in Kansas. "I don't know how to tell you this, buddy," he said, "but you don't have a canoe anymore."

"What do you mean?"

"Well, everything was going great," he said. "Then right after we crossed over into Kansas, I noticed a fly on the windshield, and somehow it was hanging on out there, even though we were doing almost seventy. Well, just as I was pointing it out to my wife, the ratchet strap we'd connected to the front of the truck flew up and disappeared, and when I looked in the side-view mirror, I saw the canoe land bolt upright behind us, fold in half, and tumble off the side of the road."

"Did you turn around?"

"Dude, no," he said. "It was broken in half."

What's really weird is that this wasn't the first canoe I'd lost. I had another one when I was in college, and someone stole it.

S: You seriously have the worst luck with canoes.

D: Tell me about it. Anyway, since we were only a few hours behind, I asked him what mile marker he'd lost it at, and he just laughed. "Yeah . . . you're not going to find it, Dan. We just pulled off to get gas, and while I was filling up, a little pickup drove by on I-70 with a big silver jackknifed canoe in the back."

I mean, seriously—that was unbelievable.

S: No, babe, that was God telling you, "Forget the canoe."

Let It Go!

D & S: It's amazing the things we hold on to.

D: I've worked for several different moving companies, and it wasn't at all uncommon for people to bring entire boxes of clothes, dishes, toys, books, and other odds and ends with them that they hadn't unpacked from the last time they moved. I'd ask, "Where would you like me to put this?"

They'd just shrug and say, "It doesn't matter. Just stick it in the closet, in the basement, or out in the garage somewhere."

I probably could have thrown the stuff away, and they wouldn't have even noticed. I mean, clearly, they felt it was important enough to bring with them, but how important could it really be if they could go years—and sometimes multiple moves—without even unpacking it?

One time we helped a guy move from Texas to Branson, and he had a full-size U-Haul truck filled with high-end antiques—I'm talking French armoires that came over on the *Mayflower* kind of antiques. It wasn't exactly my taste, but quality wise, this stuff was beautiful and could have sold at auction for tens if not hundreds of thousands of dollars.

But as soon as we got it to Branson, he had us take it straight to a storage unit. I couldn't figure out why—the house he was moving into was more than big enough to accommodate it all. And cross-country moving services aren't cheap. Why go through all the trouble and expense of transporting this stuff from Texas to Missouri if he wasn't even going to use it? So I said to the guy, "You're just gonna keep all this stuff in storage?"

FOUR TIPS FOR DECLUTTERING OR DOWNSIZING

1. If it doesn't fit, get rid of it.
2. If it's broken or parts are missing, throw it away.
3. If you haven't used it for a year, get rid of it.
4. Donate items that can still be used and are in good shape.

"Yep."

"May I ask why?"

He looked at me, dead serious, and said, "It's very valuable."

I didn't say anything, but all I could think was, *Not right now, it isn't. Right now, it's actually costing you money.*

He's not alone in this. As of 2024, the US self-storage business has mushroomed into a $44.3 billion a year industry, with the average rental cost of a single storage unit netting out at about $85 a month. That's over $1,000 a year to store things that aren't important enough to keep in the house. Over the course of a few years, this can add up to the price of a car.

S: I would like to take this opportunity to point out that my grandparents didn't charge us a penny to store those barstools.

D: Regardless, the point is that we as humans tend to go to great lengths to hold on to things we don't use.

Why We Cling to Our Things

D & S: According to bestselling author and professional tidying expert (because apparently that's a thing) Marie Kondo, there are two reasons people are unwilling or unable to let stuff go: "an attachment to the past or a fear for the future."

S: I get the attachment to the past thing—my family is big on sentimentality. My sister has kept every Christmas card she has ever been sent, and every year she puts them all out.

D: Not long ago, we were at my grandma's funeral, and my sister and aunt kept trying to give us all her old Beanie Babies and porcelain dolls "to remember her." But I don't need a tiny panda-shaped bag of beans or a little statue of a girl holding a picnic basket to remember my grandma. Those aren't the things I associate with her, anyway. When I think of her, I think about all the times we went to her house to help her roll out dough for her chicken and dumplings or the time she chased us out of the kitchen when we tried to eat her homemade cinnamon rolls before they'd cooled on the counter. It's the experiences I cherish, not the possessions.

By the same token, I don't want Canyon and Ember to need one of my old baseball caps or tackle boxes to remember me. I want them to remember all the fun times and great adventures we had together.

That's why Sam and I try not to obsess over things. We'd rather spend our money on experiences. Not only do the memories last forever, but they don't take up any space. I love my mom, but I don't need her seven-hundred-piece salt and pepper shaker collection to remember all the great times we've had together.

S: All I have to do is look at one picture of a loved one on my phone, and all the memories of that moment and that person come flooding back. We don't even save all Canyon and Ember's art projects anymore. If they make something that they're really proud of, we'll put it on the fridge for a few days, but as soon as they draw something new, we just swap it out, take a picture of the old one, and toss it.

D: I think people are afraid that if they throw out those things, they'll hurt their kids' feelings. But once kids have created something new, they typically lose interest in the old stuff. The one time Ember did get upset, we sat her down and explained that we loved her picture, but if we'd left it on the fridge, it eventually would have torn or fallen onto the floor, where our dog would have gotten it, so we took a picture of it so it will last forever. She was totally okay after that.

S: Our kids know that we value everything they create and that we're proud of them—that's what they *really* care about.

D: When I was a kid, I had a hard time getting rid of things my parents bought me. Even if I was too old to play with it, I thought, *But they worked hard to buy me that.* Now that I have kids of my own, I realize my parents probably didn't care. In fact, they were probably thrilled to get rid of the clutter.

S: I know *we* are. Every few months, I ask the kids to sort through their toys and put whatever they don't want anymore into a box for Goodwill, and they love it. As soon as I announce that it's declutter day, Canyon and Ember both race to their rooms so they can gift their old toys to kids who don't have as much as they do—and they come out with boxes full of stuff! Sometimes I'm a little surprised by what they're willing to let go of, but just because *I* feel like it should mean something to them doesn't mean it does. Besides, the whole reason we buy them toys in the first place is to give them joy. If they get more joy out of blessing someone else with it than they do playing with it, I'm 100 percent okay with that.

D: Like the professional tidying expert says, "Presents are not 'things' but a means for conveying someone's feelings. . . . You don't need to feel guilty for parting with a gift. Just thank it for the joy it gave you when you first received it."

S: That's not to say you can't keep *anything*. If there are a handful of things that genuinely mean a great deal to you, by all means, hold on to them. Just don't keep everything. I know a lot of women cringe at the thought of getting rid of their wedding dress. After all, it was such a special day, and so much time, energy, and expense went into it. But it's not the dress that made the day so special. It was what actually happened that day—the love, the union, and celebrating with friends and family—that made it special. Yet everyone feels compelled to cling to a dress they'll never wear again. And let's be honest, when was the last time you felt so nostalgic about your wedding day that you dug through the attic or crawl space to try on your old wedding dress? If you're sentimental, hang on to the garter or the veil and give the dress to charity so someone who might not be able to afford a fancy "one time only" dress can get as much enjoyment out of it as you did.

D: For me, it's the insignificant stuff that I struggle to get rid of. For example, I might have five screws left out of a box of five hundred, an old length of two-by-four,

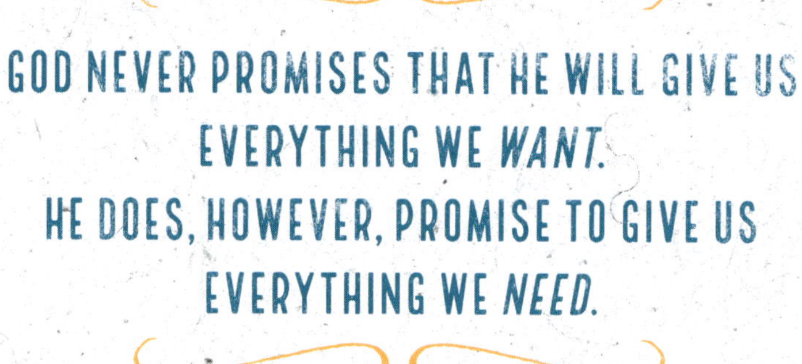

or a broken ratchet strap, and they'll sit in the back of my truck for months because I can't bring myself to throw them out. I always think, *Yeah, but I might be able to use this someday.*

S: Which brings us to the other reason Marie Kondo says we struggle to get rid of things: we're afraid. Like Dan, we think, *But what if I need this? Then what?* My mom, my sister, and I fall into this mindset with clothes. We'll go years without wearing a certain sweater, dress, or pair of shoes, but when it comes time to clean out our closets and make a pile to donate, we can't let go because, "You never know . . ." What if I give this floral sundress away and then I get invited to a summer wedding? Or what if I donate my extra pair of black heels and the strap breaks on the only pair I have left?

D: What if I toss out that Ziploc bag full of old washers and the kitchen faucet starts to leak? Or what if I give away the miter saw I never use and then Sam decides she wants crown molding in the bathroom?

S: Oh my gosh, we should totally put crown molding in the bathroom!

D: See? This is why we're afraid to get rid of stuff—even duplicate items. A few years ago, we helped Sam's sister move to Florida, and as we were helping her unpack, I noticed that she had not just one but two space heaters. When I asked her if she wanted me to get rid of them for her, she said no.

"But you live in Florida now. How about if I just get rid of one of them?"

Again, she said no. When I asked why, she said she wanted to keep them both, "just in case."

Mind you, these were not fancy space heaters. If a freak snowstorm suddenly hit southern Florida, she could have easily picked up another one for twenty dollars, but in her mind, if such an emergency *did* arise, there would be a frantic run on space heaters and she'd be left, literally, out in the cold.

S: It's that same kind of thinking that led to the great toilet paper shortage of 2020. As soon as lockdown went into effect, people started stockpiling it by the pallet for fear the country would run out. Why? I have no idea—COVID wasn't even a gastrointestinal illness. Yet there was a good nine- to ten-month stretch at the height of the pandemic when people were treating a twenty-four mega roll pack of Quilted Northern like it was worth roughly the same as a near-mint-condition '57 Chevy.

D: A few months into the pandemic, I was starting to go a little stir-crazy, so I made Canyon and Ember these novelty bed frames out of some old two-by-fours and plywood I had lying around. I made Canyon one that looked like a teepee, and I made Ember's to look like a tiny house, complete with a gabled roof. Sam thought they were really cool and suggested I make a few more and sell them online.

S: Actually, I was just trying to get rid of all that extra wood Dan was hoarding.

D: Whatever. So she posted a couple of pictures on Facebook Marketplace, and the next thing you know, some guy messaged me and wanted to know if, instead of money, he could pay me in toilet paper. I mean, seriously, who does that?

S: That would be people in the cross section of a Venn diagram who have a lifetime supply of toilet paper yet no place for their kids to sleep.

D: I mean, we joke, but strange times make people do strange things. Like when Russian hackers shut down one of the country's major fuel pipelines, causing a gas shortage up and down the East Coast. People were allegedly filling plastic bags with gasoline and storing them in their trunks and garages.

Psychologists call it panic buying, and it's basically a coping mechanism that kicks in when people experience a heightened sense of uncertainty and anxiety about the future. Granted, the toilet paper and gas hoarding are extreme examples, but they were driven by the same fundamental fear that pushes me to stockpile leftover two-by-fours and Sam to keep every article of clothing she has ever bought: the fear that God might not provide what we need when we need it.

Are You Gonna Eat That?

D & S: It's hard not to worry about the future—especially if, like us, you've spent time living from paycheck to paycheck. But take it from two people who have painted themselves into more financial corners than they can count: God is always faithful, and his blessings never run out. In fact, a big part of the reason we're willing to take so many risks is because we trust that God will provide whatever we need to get by. He has been doing it from the very beginning.

D: When the Israelites left Egypt and found themselves wandering in the desert with very little food, God literally rained honey-flavored wafers called manna down from heaven. Every morning, the Israelites would wake up and find piles of manna covering the ground. The only thing God asked was that they gather just enough to sustain them for a single day and trust that he would provide more the next morning. And then in Leviticus—

S: Seriously, babe? We're bringing Leviticus into this?

D: Yeah, I know. Most of it's brutal. But three chapters from the end, God tells Moses that when he and the other Israelites finally get to the Promised Land, they are to go ahead and work the land for six years and then take the seventh year completely off to let the land rest. "Do not plant your fields or prune your vineyards during that year," he says. "And don't store away the crops that grow on their own or gather the grapes from your unpruned vines" (Leviticus 25:4-5, NLT).

Before Moses can even ask, "Then what are we supposed to eat during that seventh year?" God essentially tells him, "Don't worry about it. I'm going to send you a special blessing, and during the sixth year, the land will produce a crop large enough to last you not just for that one year when the land is resting, but for two years after that!" (Leviticus 25:20-21).

PRACTICE A NO-SPEND MONTH

- For one whole month, try to purchase only essentials like groceries and toiletries.
- When it's someone's birthday, instead of buying a gift, make them a personalized card with a heartfelt note inside.
- Instead of going out for a meal, look up a new recipe and enjoy cooking a meal in the comfort of your home.
- When you feel the urge to make an online purchase, wait four weeks before you buy it to see if it's something you actually need.
- When you want a new outfit or a new gadget for your hobby, try asking one of your friends to see if they have a hand-me-down.
- If a friend invites you to coffee, ask them to come over instead and be your own barista.

In both instances, God provided the Israelites with exactly what they needed to survive. Yet even though bread continued to rain down from the sky every day they were in the desert, as promised, many of the Israelites hoarded a little extra, "just in case." And despite God's promise to provide a bumper crop that would sustain them for three full years, when that seventh year hit, the Israelites kept right on working the land and storing up extra wheat, grapes, and grains, "just in case."

S: Three thousand years later, we *still* don't always trust that God has our best interests at heart. We cling to our space heaters, bags of gasoline, and toilet paper with a death grip. Given the choice, we almost always opt for more. It's not enough to just "get by"—we want a safety net. We want assurance that no matter what happens, we'll be okay.

Of course, the irony is that most of us already have more than we need.

Starting from Scratch

D & S: Over the years, we've done a lot of work with Convoy of Hope, a faith-based humanitarian organization that provides food, water, and other assistance to communities in need after hurricanes, earthquakes, tornadoes, floods, and other natural disasters.

In 2022, after Hurricane Ian hit Fort Myers, Florida, we drove down to help and spent several days working at a point of distribution at a local church. All day long, people would drive through the church parking lot, and we would load up their trunks with cases of bottled water, dried goods, canned goods, cleaning supplies, hygiene kits—you name it. A lot of these people had lost virtually everything, and seeing the expressions of pure gratitude on their faces when we handed them something as simple as a bag of rice was incredibly

THE MORE YOU VALUE THINGS, THE MORE YOU HAVE TO WORK TO AFFORD THOSE THINGS.

humbling. It was a powerful reminder not only of how much we take for granted but also how little we really need to be content.

We've had the privilege of serving in a number of impoverished communities over the years, and it's always eye-opening to get perspective on the things we obsess over—like name brands. We'll gladly spend $80 on $5 worth of denim just so we can have a designer logo on the pocket, or we'll fork over $50 for a basic $6 thermos just because it's pink and "all the rage." But a child who is starving doesn't care if they're eating generic Fruity Pebbles. They're simply grateful to have something to eat. Likewise, people who have been living without a potable water supply in the wake of a hurricane aren't going to turn down a bottle of water because it isn't Evian.

Being in a place of need reminds us of what's really important, and man, does it shine a spotlight on how much excess we truly have.

D: I can't tell you how often I find myself wanting the latest hunting gear. If a new bow, trail camera, or rifle sight comes out, I feel compelled to race out and get it—even if there's nothing wrong with the one I already own.

S: It's the same with technology. We spend a fortune on the newest phone, and before we even have it paid off, we're already on the waiting list for the next one, because it has two more gigabytes of RAM or the screen is an eighth of an inch bigger.

We don't actually need these things; we just *want* them. That's what I think a lot of people get wrong about God's provision. God never promises that he will give us everything we *want*. He does, however, promise to give us everything we *need*. And what he wants us to need most is him. We, on the other hand, want to be comfortable. And the more comfortable we are, the less we need God.

D: That's why when Jesus sent his disciples out to spread his message, he told them not to bring anything with them other than a walking stick and the clothes on their backs. He wanted them to learn how to depend on God for everything.

The funny thing is, you would think that having very little would be terrifying, but it can actually be freeing.

The High Cost of Clutter

S: When we left Colorado, we went from living in a nine-hundred-square-foot two-bedroom apartment to a two-hundred-square-foot trailer—and, lest you forget, there were four of us.

By the time we finished "decluttering," we had gotten rid of roughly 80 percent of what we owned. All we took with us were whatever clothes we could each fit in a small laundry basket (about five changes of clothes each, plus a winter coat, scarf, and gloves), a handful of pots and pans, four forks, four knives, four spoons, four plates, four bowls, four cups, a few cooking utensils, one set of sheets for us and one for each of the kids, two sets of bath towels, a handful of toiletries, a couple of odds and ends, and two or three of the kids' favorite toys. And do you know what? We didn't miss a single thing. All the clothes, furniture, toys, and gadgets we once considered indispensable were almost instantly forgotten. Within two weeks of leaving Colorado, we couldn't even tell you what we'd left behind.

As an added bonus, because we had less stuff, there was also much less to clean. Honestly, until we lived in the trailer, I had no idea how much time I'd spent every day tidying up—putting away toys, organizing closets, straightening cupboards, doing dishes and putting them away, watering plants, vacuuming, mopping, dusting, doing the laundry, and folding and ironing clothes. I never realized it before, but the more stuff you have, the more time and energy you have to spend taking care of all of it.

D: This is especially true when it comes to big-ticket items like cars or boats or motorcycles. It's easy to invest hundreds, if not thousands, of hours (not to mention small fortunes) maintaining and upgrading vehicles. The same goes for pools and property. If we're not intentional, we'll find ourselves spending the weekend mowing, edging, weeding, and watering the lawn; chasing leaves around the pool with one of those giant nets; and fussing with chlorine levels—and that's to say nothing about hot tub upkeep.

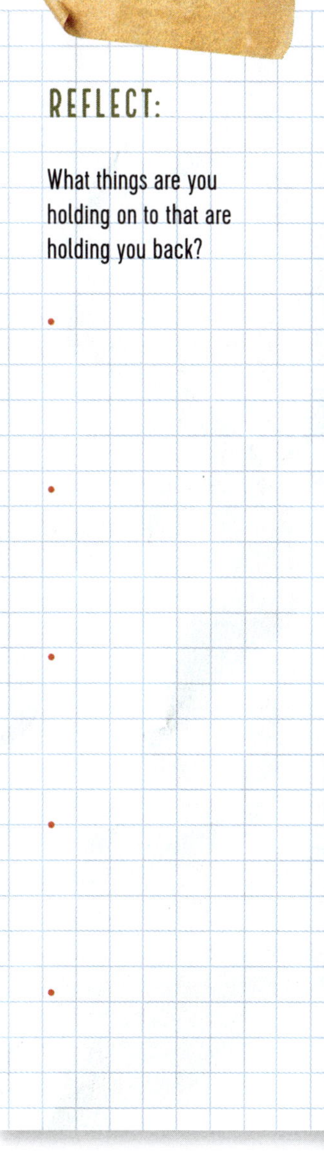

S: And it's not just a question of physical clutter. There's also a lot of emotional clutter that comes with having too much stuff. I call it the mess-stress correlation.

Because my mom had to work so much when we were growing up, our house was always a little on the messy side. Justine and I both had a lot of toys and—when we got older—clothes, and since none of us were too keen on cleaning or organizing, we just got used to having dirty dishes in the sink and stepping over and around things.

The summer before Dan and I got married, I worked as a nanny for a couple with two kids, and their home was immaculate. There was a place for everything, and everything was always in its place. When the parents left in the morning, the breakfast dishes were done and put away, there were fresh hand towels in the bathroom, and you could walk freely from room to room without tripping over anything. Just a few days into my job, it struck me how peaceful it was and how much more relaxed I felt when I was there. Just knowing where everything was and not having to deal with the sensory overload of stuff piled up everywhere made me feel calmer and happier. To this day, whenever the kids have too many toys out at once or Dan leaves his clothes on the furniture, I can feel my stress level kick up a couple of notches.

D: Ultimately, it all comes down to what you value and how you want to live. We decided early on that we would much rather spend our money on experiences instead of things. For months now, Canyon has been asking for a Nintendo Switch,

WHEN YOU SHIFT YOUR THINKING TO SEEING TIME AS CURRENCY, ALL YOUR PRIORITIES CHANGE.

but not only do those cost a lot of money, we know that if we buy him one, he'll sit in his room all day playing it by himself. We'd prefer to spend the money on a trip to the zoo or the aquarium or to play miniature golf as a family. These are memories we can carry for years to come as opposed to one more toy or gadget the kids will play with for a couple of weeks and then dump in the back of the closet or the bottom of a drawer.

We also want them to be creative and find ways to entertain themselves instead of being reliant on TV or video games for amusement. A couple of weeks ago, we had to replace one of our rugs, and the new one came wrapped around an eight-foot-long cardboard tube, so I cut it in half and gave each kid a four-foot piece. They spent hours playing with them, pretending they were Ninjas and using them like giant swords and then pretending they were on a safari and using them like walking sticks. When that got old, they raced Canyon's toy cars through them and then imagined they were spying on each other through telescopes. It was awesome.

S: It's not that we don't buy our kids toys—we do. But more often than not, they have more fun playing with random stuff they find around the house. They love making things out of empty toilet paper rolls and old delivery boxes. Frankly, we've yet to find any toy that brings our kids as much joy as the blankets from their beds. They are forever making blanket forts in the living room, wearing them like capes or Jedi robes, or scrunching them up like balls and tossing them across the room to one another. Part of the reason our kids have such active imaginations is because we *don't* have a lot of stuff, and we love that!

D: We also want to be able to pick up and go at a moment's notice and have the freedom to pursue different employment opportunities—and the more stuff you have weighing you down, the harder that is to do.

As a former mover, I can assure you that the sheer cost of moving rooms full of furniture, books, clothes, dishes, knickknacks, and other miscellaneous stuff cross-country is astronomical—never mind the stress of trying to find another place big enough to accommodate all of it. We want to be agile and remain open to whatever exciting adventures God brings our way.

S: Most importantly, we want our kids to value experiences over things, to be generous with their time and resources, to have adventurous spirits, and to put their trust in the Lord and follow wherever he leads. We don't want them to grow up obsessed with material possessions, because that's where the cycle starts. The more you value things, the more you have to work to afford those things.

D: The reality is, it's possible to work yourself to death so you can afford a big house, fancy cars, expensive clothes, high-end furniture, giant TVs, and other big-ticket items, and then not have time to relax and enjoy them. The less emphasis you place on possessions, the less money you need. And let's face it: at the end of the day, a lot of what we spend our money on is optional.

S: Simplifying your life and de-emphasizing the importance of material possessions means less time spent working and more time to spend with family and friends. Because when you're content getting by with less, you're free to do so much more.

D: We're not saying money isn't important—we just believe that time spent with family and friends is more important. You can always make more money, but once time is gone, it's gone. There's no getting it back. That's what makes it so valuable. When you shift your thinking to seeing time as currency, all your priorities change.

If downsizing taught us nothing else, it's how little we actually need—not just to get by but to be genuinely happy.

S: It's funny, when we got back to Missouri, everyone kept asking us, "What can we get for you? What do you need?" It seemed impossible that we could be so content with so little.

D: For us, a safety net isn't so much about finances as it is about relationships. Our most important safety nets are the Lord and each other. Those were our only constants through all the financial hardships and challenges we faced in Colorado, and in the end, they were all we really needed. Everything else managed to take care of itself.

Speaking of safety nets, it will probably come as no surprise that I'm a huge fan of those reality shows where they drop a bunch of outdoor enthusiasts in the middle of the Canadian wilderness with nothing but a multipurpose knife, some fishing line, a tarp, a small hatchet, and a piece of flint and see who can last the longest. It never ceases to amaze me how people can take next to nothing and somehow build a shelter, make a fire, and catch enough fish to survive for months all alone in the middle of nowhere. Yet that's all *any* of us really need to survive: food, water, fire, shelter, God, and each other.

And maybe a canoe.

THE KEY TO LIVING A

Life of Adventure

IS TO FOCUS ON

Experiences,

NOT THINGS.

9

SOMETIMES You Just Gotta Wing It

D & S: "You guys are moving *again*?"

"Dan quit his job?"

"You're living in an RV?"

"Sam wants to do *what*?"

"Do you guys have any idea what you're doing?"

Honestly, most of the time we don't know what we're doing. We just kind of figure it out as we go. Sometimes it works out (like moving to Colorado), and sometimes it doesn't (like actually *living* in Colorado). But that's okay—part of choosing adventure is being willing to make it work on the fly. We've pretty much gotten used to people questioning the decisions we make. But even we were a little surprised by how strongly our friends and family reacted to our decision to go into social media.

To a certain extent, we got it. When we first decided to get into social media full-time, "influencer" was one of the most popular career aspirations for our generation. But while a lot of people were trying it, very few were making a successful living doing it. Naturally, we got hit with questions like, "What if it doesn't work out?" "How are you going to provide for your family?" "What if you run out of stuff to post about?" or "What are you going to do if people stop following you?"

And, of course, our favorite: "You have two kids. Shouldn't at least one of you have a *real* job?" We still get that one!

D: What a lot of people don't realize is that being a full-time influencer *is* a real job. They think it's just posting the occasional picture of something we had for dinner or something we just bought or made, along with a little emoji and maybe some background music. They have no idea how much work goes into this job. In fact, it's not at all unusual for us—and when I say us, I mean Sam—to spend more hours working on our social media accounts than either of us ever did working a regular nine-to-five job.

When we first started, we didn't realize that either.

From Hobby to Hustle

S: At first, I *was* just posting the occasional picture or story about my day-to-day life. It wasn't anything earth-shattering—just little stuff like going on a walk with the kids, doing laundry, or Canyon helping me with the dishes. I just did it because it was fun—and it gave me a much-needed creative outlet.

Then I shared about the RV renovation, and more and more people started following me. It was just a couple hundred or so, but then I noticed that some of the people following me had tens or even hundreds of thousands of people following them. So I started poking around their accounts to see what they were doing, and it turned out that in addition to their regular posts and reels, they were also advertising products attached to whatever they were posting about. And here's the real kicker—they were being paid for it!

I thought, *Wait a minute . . . I could actually make money doing this?* So I literally googled "how to make money as an influencer" and found all kinds of information about creating partnerships with

different brands and negotiating product-for-post deals and commission fees—and it looked totally doable! I started reaching out to different companies and brands that Dan and I were already using, like Lowe's and Home Depot, and asking if they would be interested in partnering with us. Because I didn't have a ton of followers yet, it was a little hit or miss, and the few companies that did respond were smaller product-for-post deals, where they gave us a free product in exchange for posting a video about it. For example, Walex gave us a bunch of deodorizing toilet tabs for our RV, which might not sound very exciting, but since it was something we actually used, at least we didn't have to buy them for a while.

One day Dan's cousin reached out to me. "Hey, there's this online mobile banking app called Chime," he told us. "They're giving away $100 Amazon gift cards in exchange for referrals." We both set up accounts, and sure enough, they sent each of us a $100 gift card. As an added bonus, Dan and I really liked the app and started using the credit card.

Flash forward a few weeks: Chime posted on their Instagram stories that they were looking for members to create little videos about why they love the Chime credit card. If your story was picked, you got—you guessed it—a $100 Amazon gift card. While we were swimming in toilet tabs, there were plenty of other things still sitting in our cart, so I made a note to put something together with Dan later that week. One thing led to another, and we completely forgot about it. That Friday, I was dropping Dan off at the airport, and just as he was about to step out of the car, I said, "Oh, shoot, babe, we never did that video."

He said, "Well, let's just do it right now."

Mind you, I'd been sick all week and didn't have any makeup on, but $100 is $100, so you'd better believe I whipped that phone right out of my purse.

"Okay, I'll go first," I told Dan. "Then I'll kick it over to you. All you have to do is talk about your favorite feature of the card, got it?"

"Yep."

I hit record, and with as much professionalism as I could muster sitting in the departures lane at DIA in an unwashed T-shirt and pajama bottoms, I said, "Hi! We're Sam and Dan Mathews, and we love using the Chime mobile app. My favorite thing about banking with Chime is that every morning they let us know exactly how much is in our account, and every time a new transaction posts, we get an alert." Then I turned the camera on Dan, and he said, "My favorite feature of the Chime debit card is the rounded corners. It never gets stuck in my pocket."

Seriously, that had to be the most pointless thing you could have possibly said.

D: No, it wasn't.

S: Babe, *every* debit card has rounded corners!

D: Oh, you loved it.

S: He's not wrong. I immediately started cracking up. And since he had a flight to catch, we didn't have time to do another one, so I just sent it in—no makeup, idiotic rounded corners comment, and all. And wouldn't you know, the next day I got an email from Chime telling me how much their marketing team loved our video, along with a $100 Amazon gift card.

D: Told ya.

S: A couple of months later, I got another email from the head of Chime's marketing department asking if we'd be willing to make a few more videos and promising us an Amazon gift card for each one they ended up using. We made three more, and because they had liked the first one so much, we did kinda the same schtick, where I was the straight man and Dan said or did something goofy. They took all three!

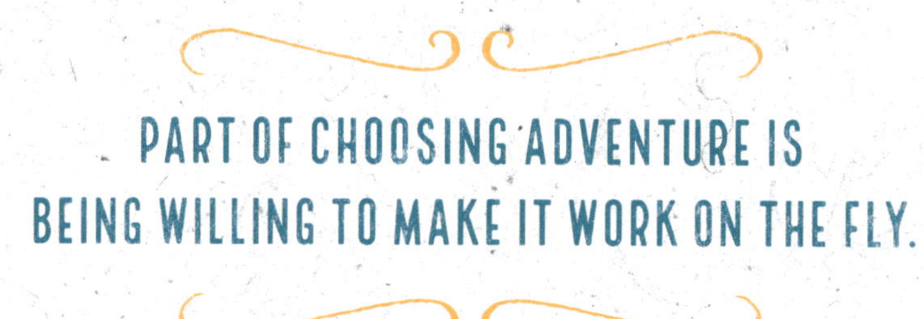

A while later, they emailed us again and asked for a few more. I told Dan, "They think you're hilarious, and they're accepting everything we send. Why don't we send a whole bunch of them and see what happens?"

We had a blast making up a ton of different skits about how we used the card and the mobile app, most of which centered around our RV. When all was said and done, we probably sent them thirty videos, and they took every one. We ended up getting several thousand dollars' worth of Amazon gift cards.

D: It was definitely a step up from a free carton of toilet tabs.

S: I said to the marketing guy, "Listen, if you ever have any other opportunities, please let us know."

"Funny you should say that," he said. "We've actually been thinking about doing a series of commercials with some of our Chime members, and we'd love for you guys to do one."

A few months later, Chime sent a camera crew out to Missouri, and Dan and I filmed a one-minute commercial about the different features of the card and how it helped us get our small RV renovation business off the ground. They filmed it outside, and it was freezing, but they got some great footage of the work we'd done on the RV. Not only did the exposure boost our social media presence, but the money we made from the commercial helped us pay down a lot of the debt we'd accrued since moving to Colorado. And it all started with Dan and me basically winging it in our simple response to a marketing email.

D: That's when Sam really kicked it into high gear.

S: I started researching what kinds of things brands look for in content creators, how I could reach out to corporate partners, and what I could do with our Instagram, YouTube, and TikTok accounts to make us more attractive to them.

I also started keeping track of which of our videos were getting the most views, which ones garnered the most comments and had the highest viewer engagement, and which ones were the most frequently shared. This helped me better understand what our followers liked and what they wanted to see. I wanted to make sure our followers were getting exactly what they wanted, and I knew that the more followers we had, the more attractive we would be to brands.

Having said that, it was never just about the partnerships for us. A big part of what I love about working in social media is coming up with new things to talk about and creative things to do. I don't want to be a pitchwoman who is constantly hurling products at people. Dan and I love doing little stunts and skits. Not only is it more fun, but it also feels more authentic if the partnerships grow organically out of something we're already doing.

D: Make no mistake: Sam is the brains behind all this. I'm just the cart guy. Honestly, she could have a degree in social media with the amount of time she has put into researching algorithms, the most effective days and times to post, what's trending, and how people respond to a seven-second video compared to a forty-nine-second video. It's an insane amount of work to "organically" grow a social media platform.

S: It also takes an insane amount of time. It was easily two and a half years before we were able to earn a consistent, livable income online, in part because we were feeling our way through it, mostly by trial and error. And there were *a lot* of errors. The worst one came on June 2, 2020.

Timing Is Everything

S: As it happened, our decision to dive headfirst into the world of social media happened right about the same time as the pandemic. A few months prior, I had created an e-book for brides on how to plan their wedding. At that point, I had almost ten years of experience as a wedding coordinator, and since we were looking for ways to generate revenue online, I figured I could share some of what I'd learned and see if we could make a couple of extra bucks.

Dan and I went to Panera with our laptops with the plan to officially launch the e-book, and while we were thinking through exactly what we wanted to say, I posted a little video of Dan and the kids kicking around the soccer ball.

What we didn't realize was that that particular Tuesday had been declared Blackout Tuesday, and—as a show of solidarity with the Black community in the wake of George Floyd's murder—everyone was encouraged to post a black square on their social media page and not post anything else for the day to provide space for the oppressed and marginalized to speak.

Within minutes of our posting the video, a message popped up on my screen:

> How dare you not quiet yourself for the oppressed!

I didn't even know what that meant. I apologized and asked what they were talking about. By the time I realized what was going on, our socials were lighting up with people who couldn't believe I'd had the audacity to post a video of my kids playing with their dad on Blackout Tuesday.

D: Sam had quit her job with Convoy of Hope three days earlier to pursue social media full-time, and literally on her first post, this happened. And people were *really* coming after her. People were flat out calling us racists and white supremacists. It didn't matter that we were unaware there was an online movement taking place.

S: Even when we apologized, people kept attacking us. We ended up losing 10 percent of our followers.

D: It didn't take long for us to realize that there was no point in even trying to defend ourselves—there was just no winning on this. That's why early on, we decided it's not productive for us to read all the comments people leave on our socials, though sometimes Sam can't help herself.

S: I do like interacting with people, and for the most part, the comments are kind. But heaven help you if something you say or do unintentionally sets someone off. A couple of times a year, it affects me to the point where I have to walk away from

TIPS FOR GETTING STARTED IN SOCIAL MEDIA

- Know your audience.
- Choose your platforms.
- Develop a regular posting schedule.
- Create engaging content.
- Set regular goals.
- Collaborate with others.
- Be authentic to who you are; don't try to be someone else.

our accounts for a few days. Even though I know that what I post comes from a place of love, I can't help but take it personally—especially when it's an attack on my character. I constantly have to remind myself who I am, and whose I am, and that my value doesn't come from someone else's opinions.

D: And I often have to remind Sam that the people who are lashing out are only seeing a ten-second, maybe twenty-second, slice of our lives. They don't have the complete picture, nor do we necessarily owe it to them.

S: It's still hard, because I sometimes feel the need to justify myself when people call me a bad mom who doesn't spend enough time with her kids simply because they don't see them online.

D: This is also ridiculous. For one thing, Canyon doesn't want to be recorded, and we're not going to force him to do it. Ember doesn't mind it, but the truth is, we film most of our videos during the day while they're at school—first, because it's a lot quieter, and second, because getting all our online content out of the way while they're at school means we're free to give them our undivided attention when they get home.

S: When we decided to go on social media, we vowed to share every aspect of our lives—the good, the bad, the ugly, the hard, and the joyful. Before we went live with wearedanandsam.com, I spent a lot of time scrolling through Instagram and TikTok, and I noticed that a lot of the professional influencers had very specific niches. Some were about gluten-free baking; others were about farmsteading, interior decorating, or DIY-ing. This makes sense, because when you narrow your focus, it's easier to figure out who your audience is and what they're looking for. But I really didn't want to put us in a box where we could only talk about one thing day in and day out. I wanted to be able to share whatever we happened to be focusing on during any given season—and as you might have guessed, we jump around a lot.

At first, we focused mostly on our home life with the kids. Then we got the RV, and I started documenting the renovation process. When we started our surrogacy journey, we talked about that. And even those topics weren't exclusive. When we

were in the middle of the RV renovation, for example, I still posted random stuff about the kids or other things Dan and I were doing. Ultimately, we just share about our life—whatever it happens to look like on any given day.

D: That's why we decided to call our accounts #wearedanandsam. We tossed around some catchier, more creative titles and hashtags related to RVs and travel, but we knew our lives would be constantly changing, so we needed something that would stand the test of time.

S: Whether we're in the middle of a surrogacy journey, flipping RVs, traveling the country, or just hanging out at home with our kids, we'll always be Dan and Sam.

D: As long as we feel like the Lord is leading us to share our lives online, we will continue to follow his lead—even if we end up stepping on a few toes every now and then. Because you never know where a simple post might lead.

One Thing Leads to Another

D & S: Part of the fun of flying by the seat of your pants is how quickly one adventure can turn into another.

Not long after we sold our RV, a friend who had been following our renovation process online reached out to us. "Hey, my parents have an old RV that they don't use anymore. It's half gutted, and we've been trying to sell it, but everyone wants a fully finished one. What would you guys think about renovating and selling it for us and keeping the profit?"

Needless to say, we were stoked. While we had turned a small profit on our first RV, we didn't have enough money to buy another one to flip. So to be given free rein to renovate someone else's vehicle was a dream come true. We ended up putting about $5,000 of our own money into the renovation, but then we sold it for $15,000, so we doubled our investment—and we had a blast doing it!

S: Just like the first time, I spent a lot of time looking at what other people in the RV life community were doing with their vehicles. That's when I noticed that several people were doing something called "client flips," where a client pays you up front to do the renovation, and after they sell it, they give you a cut of the profit. That was even better for us, because it didn't require us to put any of our own money in up front—just our time.

D: Sam put the offer out there, and we ended up doing back-to-back client flips. We even ended up flipping a houseboat!

It was awesome. We were our own bosses. We worked as many or as few hours as we wanted to each week, and we were able to spend a ton of time with the kids.

S: Of course, not every investment panned out. I found one RV online that the owners were selling for just $7,000, and I figured we could invest a few thousand upgrading the interior and turn it around for a quick profit.

D: But once we started gutting it, we ran into a lot of undisclosed water damage. The whole thing ended up being a nightmare, because the seller wouldn't own up to it. And since the damage was preexisting, our insurance wouldn't cover it either. When all was said and done, we ended up losing almost $6,000 on it.

S: The funny thing is, when we first went to look at it, neither of us felt good about it. I was sick as a dog, but we'd driven over an hour and a half to see it.

D: And Sam being Sam, she didn't want to hurt the couple's feelings by backing out, so we went ahead with the purchase.

S: As a business venture, it was a failure. But it was also a great learning experience and underscored for us the importance of trusting our gut and not moving forward if we don't feel peace about the situation.

D: That's the thing about winging it—it's not always going to work. And that's okay. Sometimes our mistakes are the very things that God uses to help us learn and grow. But even when we fail, God is still sovereign. He still has a plan for our lives, and a stupid decision on our part isn't going to change that. In fact, I genuinely believe our failures can put us right where we need to be, because failure makes us vulnerable, and it's when we're feeling the most vulnerable that we're most likely to turn to God for help.

Were we in a spot where we could afford to lose $6,000? No. Did it completely ruin us financially? Again, no. Have we moved forward with any other business decisions without feeling peace about it since?

S: Not on your life!

D: More importantly, we didn't let that mistake stop us from stepping out of our comfort zone, taking chances, and trying new things.

Of course, we all make mistakes when we're trying something we've never done before. That's how we learn. Sam and I didn't know anything about being influencers when we started—and we stepped in it big-time. But we didn't quit. We stuck with it, learned more, and figured it out.

S: We'd never renovated an RV before either. We'd never even used a paint sprayer—and we made a royal mess of that too. But we figured it out. If we'd let inexperience or the fear of making a mistake stop us from trying new things, we never would have bought that first RV to begin with—and look where it led!

D: What started out as a wild idea on Sam's part ended up turning into a successful business that not only helped us get back to Missouri and pay down our debt but also ended up launching our career as influencers and allowing us to achieve our dream of working for ourselves. I can promise you, neither of us saw that coming! But God did. We just had to trust him—even when we had no idea what lay ahead.

S: As an added bonus, all the flipping and networking we did during that season helped set up one of the most amazing adventures we've ever had. Oddly enough, once again, it all started with me looking for a way to manage my postpartum emotions.

Special Delivery

S: We were matched with our intended parents shortly after we moved back to Missouri. In fact, we did the embryo transfer the same week we filmed the Chime commercial.

For the most part, the entire pregnancy went smoothly, though I did experience terrible morning sickness, which I never had when I was carrying Canyon and Ember. I don't know whether the fertility meds played a role in that, but suffice it to say, even though I'd already delivered two of our own kids, Dan and I still felt like we were flying by the seat of our pants with that pregnancy.

D: We had no idea how Sam's body would react to all the shots and the meds or if her system would reject a foreign embryo. Plus, we'd never gone through a pregnancy with another couple before, so having someone else speaking into Sam's pregnancy decisions and being present at many of her doctor appointments and in the delivery room was a new experience for us too.

S: And, of course, there was the whole question of how our kids would handle the idea of the baby in their mommy's tummy not coming home with us—or, for that matter, how *I* would handle the postpartum experience. So even though we put a great deal of thought and prayer into deciding to become surrogates, once the embryo transfer took place, we were basically just along for the ride.

Everything revolved around August 4, my due date. Since I had virtually no postpartum symptoms with Canyon and only a handful of blue days with Ember, we were optimistic. Still, everything about this journey felt different, and this time

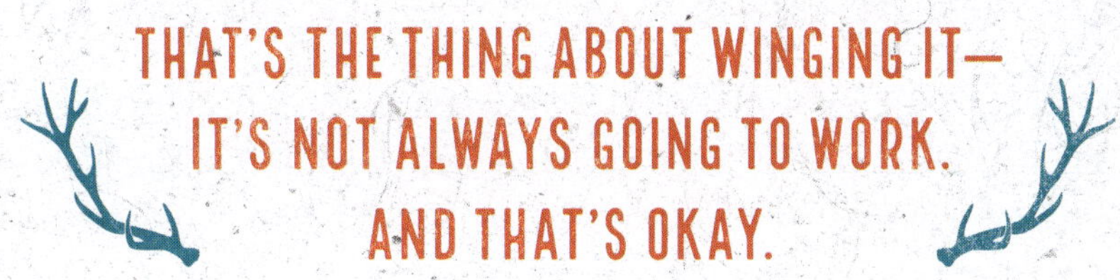

I wouldn't have the distraction of a newborn at home. So that summer, Dan and I started talking about what we could do immediately following the delivery to take my mind off everything.

D: We kicked around going to Hawaii or the Bahamas or maybe even Jamaica—someplace we'd never been before. We wanted to give Sam a change of scenery and focus on us as a family for a couple of weeks.

S: In mid-June, Camping World reached out to us. I had been messaging back and forth with them for almost a year, trying to convince them to partner with us. By that point, we'd renovated five RVs, and thanks to the Chime commercial, our following had grown exponentially—especially within the RV life community. Plus, ever since we sold the RV we had returned to Missouri in, we'd been staying with either friends or my mom, so I was really hoping they'd be open to leasing us something big enough for the four of us to live in for several months in exchange for posting about it online. Now that we finally had a sizable following, they were in!

D: Our plan was to pick up the RV a week or so after Sam's delivery date so she could have some time to heal. Then we'd head to Wisconsin to spend a few days with my family before heading out West.

S: We wanted to go to Yellowstone, Yosemite, and Mount Rushmore, and we had some friends in Utah we wanted to visit.

D: We figured we'd camp out in the national parks and flat-tow our truck behind us so we could go on day trips. We weren't overly concerned about nailing down the specifics—after all, we had plenty of time to get ready.

S: Then I delivered a full week early. I went in for my thirty-eight-week checkup, and the doctor said that while the baby was perfectly healthy, the numbers weren't quite what they wanted to see on the nonstress test. Since I was practically at thirty-nine weeks, they decided it would be in the baby's best interest for me to be induced that day.

The intended parents and I went across the parking lot to the hospital while Dan ran home to get my overnight bag. A few hours later, Dan held one of my hands, the intended mom held the other, and the intended dad cut the cord. Just like that, our first surrogacy journey came to its beautiful conclusion.

D: Sam was amazing. It really was awesome to be there and see the intended parents meet their child for the first time. It's never been easy watching Sam go through so much pain, but seeing the parents hold their baby took me back to the first time I held Canyon and Ember. I know Sam always says she loves labor and delivery, and while I might not get the first part of that, I can definitely see why she loves the second.

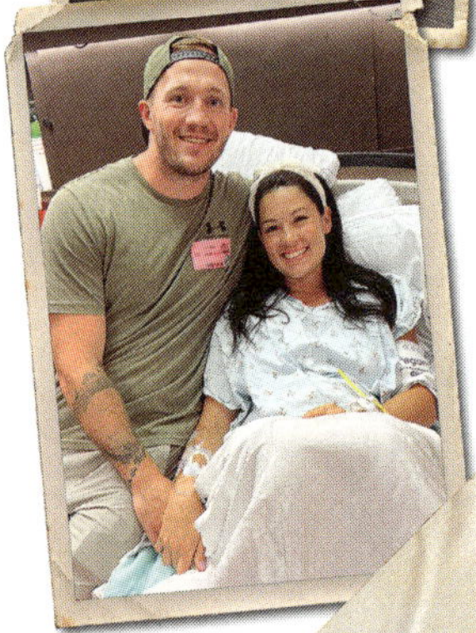

S: Truth be told, I had forgotten how exhausting—and frankly, excruciating—labor is, but to see the mom, dad, and baby together after all those years of pain and loss made every second of it worthwhile.

Before we were discharged the next day, we had a chance to meet and hold the baby. I didn't feel the need to hold him for a long time; I just wanted to see what I'd been a part of and get some closure. And in case you're wondering, he was adorable. But at that point, all I really wanted to do was go home and see *our* kids.

There was only one problem.

My mom had taken Canyon and Ember to California to spend a couple of weeks visiting extended family so I could have some time to get ready for the delivery and then recover for a few days without them underfoot. I hadn't anticipated how badly I would want to see them when I got home. It was just so strange coming home without a baby *and* not being able to see my own kids.

Thankfully, my mom was able to get a flight back the next day. As soon as they got back, we took them to the Airbnb where the intended parents were staying so they could meet the baby and get a little closure of their own.

They were young, but they understood what was happening. Every day, Ember would pet my belly and talk to the baby. I would let them feel the baby kick, and they both loved to blow raspberries kisses for the baby on my belly. We never used the words *brother* or *sister*. They had met the intended parents, and they knew the baby belonged to them and I was just carrying him for them until he was born. But we still didn't know how they would react to my belly suddenly being gone and not getting to interact with the baby they'd been talking to for the past nine months.

We weren't there long, but they got to see the baby and play with his little toes. Even though they were too little to articulate what was happening or fully process it, I think it was good for them to see the intended parents with their baby.

After we left the Airbnb, Dan and I gave each of the kids a little gift from the baby, because the research we'd done said this would help them transition a little easier. It did—or at the very least, it distracted them. I focused all my energy on them and on helping them not dwell on the fact that this baby wasn't coming home with us. For the most part, they did great. They occasionally asked about the baby—how old he was and how big he was now—but then, like most kids their age, their minds quickly moved on to other things.

Even I did better than expected. A few days after we got home, I got hit with the same postpartum blues I'd experienced after Ember was born, but this was quickly overshadowed by the excitement of hitting the open road. Dan and I had been talking about traveling the country full-time in an RV for years, and it was finally happening!

D: Thanks to Sam's early delivery, it was happening fast.

The Trip of a Lifetime

D: From the day Sam got home from the hospital, we had fourteen days to pack for the next six months, map out a rough itinerary, load all our stuff into the RV, figure out how to set up a flat-tow, and—oh yeah, buy a truck.

S: That was our first little surprise. We had picked up a used Toyota Tundra after our Denali was stolen, but as Dan was reading up on the motor home we were getting, he discovered that there are only two truck models capable of being flat-towed: the Ford F-150 and the Chevy Silverado. So now, on top of everything else, we had some last-minute truck shopping to do.

D: And Sam was still recovering physically from delivery, so there was a lot going on.

S: It *was* a bit chaotic, but it was exactly the distraction I needed.

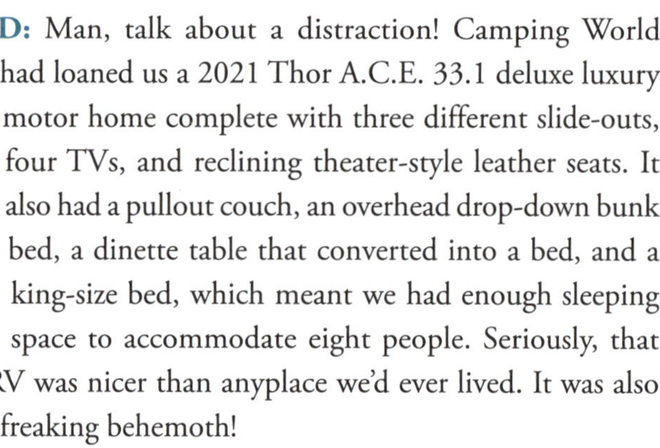

D: Man, talk about a distraction! Camping World had loaned us a 2021 Thor A.C.E. 33.1 deluxe luxury motor home complete with three different slide-outs, four TVs, and reclining theater-style leather seats. It also had a pullout couch, an overhead drop-down bunk bed, a dinette table that converted into a bed, and a king-size bed, which meant we had enough sleeping space to accommodate eight people. Seriously, that RV was nicer than anyplace we'd ever lived. It was also a freaking behemoth!

The vehicle itself was just over thirty-four feet long, plus we were flat-towing an eighteen-foot Silverado behind us, and the hookup system for that was at least four feet. If that wasn't ridiculous enough, we also had a hitch attached to the back of the Silverado to carry our e-bikes. So the overall length was roughly sixty feet—the length of a bowling lane. It was basically the equivalent of

THERE'S SOMETHING ABOUT BREAKING AWAY FROM YOUR USUAL ROUTINE AND TRYING SOMETHING NEW THAT BREATHES FRESH LIFE INTO YOU.

driving an 18-wheeler. Plus, the thing weighed more than 18,000 pounds! I'd driven the school bus, but I wasn't flat-towing another full-size truck behind it, and the bus had been fully gutted, so it was only a fraction of the weight.

S: Here's a fun fact: even though a motor home can be roughly the same size as an 18-wheeler, because it's not a commercial vehicle, you don't need a special license to operate one. Or apparently, even a lesson. That was our second little surprise.

D: When we went to pick up the motor home, we were given a full tutorial on how to lower the bunk beds, how to work the slide-outs, how to hook up the water and propane tanks, and how to put out the awnings—but as far as actually *driving* was concerned, they basically said, "Be careful. It's big. Try not to hit anything."

S: Fortunately, Dan managed to make it all the way back to my mom's house without doing too much damage.

D: I popped up on a bunch of curbs, backed into a road sign, and took out a few low-hanging tree branches, but for the most part, I got the hang of it. Then I set up the flat-tow—which turned out to be a lovely ten-step process in itself—attached the Silverado, and helped Sam get all our stuff loaded, and we hit the road.

S: Our first stop was a local KOA campsite just outside Springfield. Because all the RVs we'd flipped had been tow-behinds, this was the first time we'd lived in or tried to maneuver something with its own engine. So we thought it might be a good idea to spend a few days getting familiar with it before taking off on the 640-mile drive to see Dan's family in Wisconsin.

D: It didn't really matter. From the second we crossed into Illinois, our entire route was under construction, so I was basically white-knuckling my way through a single narrow lane with concrete barriers to my right and oncoming vehicles to my left the entire time.

At one point, I got stuck behind a semi and actually swerved over onto the shoulder to pass him. He laid on the horn and flipped me the bird. Meanwhile, Sam was sitting next to me uploading pictures and videos onto Instagram, and I was sitting there in a puddle of my own sweat, going, "Um, babe, could you maybe help me a little here? I need to get back over, and I can't see a thing."

Illinois was just the start. A few weeks later, when we were crossing the plains of South Dakota, the wind would pick up so much, we might as well have had sails on that thing. We kept getting blown into the other lane, and there were a couple of times when we were almost blown right off the road. For the better part of two hundred miles, I didn't even blink.

S: Dan sat there with an absolute death grip on the wheel, saying, "Nobody talk to me" for miles.

D: When we were driving through Northern California, we had to wind our way down a steep mountain road with nothing but a four-foot metal railing between us and a five-hundred-foot drop-off to the canyon below. It was like that for forty-five miles. You could literally smell our brakes burning as we inched our way down. I was sure they were going to fail at any second, and we were just gonna crash through the railing and plummet to our deaths.

S: Needless to say, when Dan asked, "Hey, do you want to take a turn driving?" I said, "Absolutely not!"

D: Sixteen thousand miles, and Sam didn't take the wheel once.

S: I did too!

D: Oh, I'm sorry. Sixteen thousand miles, and Sam took the wheel twice—for all of about two minutes.

Here's the thing. Normally, I'm pretty good at holding it, but the gas tank on this thing was so huge, we could go several hundred miles between stops. There were two times I really had to pee, but I didn't wanna pull over. So I said, "Babe, I need you to take the wheel for a couple minutes while I run back and use the restroom."

Sam replied, "No way! I'm not driving this thing!"

I told her, "We're on a straightaway in the middle of nowhere. There's no traffic for miles. All you have to do is stay between the lines." She just stared at me like I'd sprouted a second head. Well, I really had to go, so I said, "All right, look. I'm gonna unbuckle my seat belt and flip up the armrest. I have the cruise control on, so as soon as I slide out, you slide in, okay?"

S: Once Dan was out of the seat, I panicked. I slid over and grabbed the wheel, and the next thing I knew, he was just gone, and I was sitting there, gripping the wheel for dear life.

D: I kid you not, I wasn't in the bathroom for ten seconds when I heard, "Get back here quick! There's a semi coming behind me, and I don't wanna crash!" Now, how we were going to crash into a semi that was a good three hundred yards behind us, I have no idea, but she sounded so panicked that I zipped back up and just held it.

Twice during that trip, I asked Sam to take the wheel so I could run to the bathroom, and she managed to keep it together for all of a quarter of a mile before frantically calling me back up front. Suffice it to say, by the time we returned that motor home six months later, I had the bladder control of a Jedi master.

REFLECT:

List three things you have always wanted to try but haven't yet.

1.

2.

3.

S: Smoking brake pads and sweat aside, we really did have a fantastic time.

D: We literally had no idea where we were going. There were times we'd still be driving at two or three in the morning because we couldn't decide where we wanted to stop. And pretty much everywhere we *did* stop was awesome.

In South Dakota, before you get into Badlands National Park, you drive up a nondescript dirt road, and it looks like you're just driving off into a field. Then all of a sudden, the ground in front of you disappears and you find yourself right on the rim, overlooking miles of canyons, ridges, pinnacles, and buttes that have been there practically since the beginning of time. I parked the RV about six feet from the edge, and when we walked out our front door the next morning, we were met by one of the most spectacular sunrises we'd ever seen—not to mention a herd of bighorn sheep grazing less than five yards away. Canyon and Ember lost their ever-loving minds.

S: They had an absolute blast. They became junior rangers at all the national parks, and whenever we stopped, we'd let them pick up a rock, an acorn, a snakeskin, or some other little treasure, and we'd help them research what it was. Then they'd tape it to a piece of paper, label it, and write something they learned about it. It might not have been a traditional preschool or kindergarten curriculum, but they got to visit twenty-six states, and they learned all about the different plants, trees, flowers, and animals in each of them.

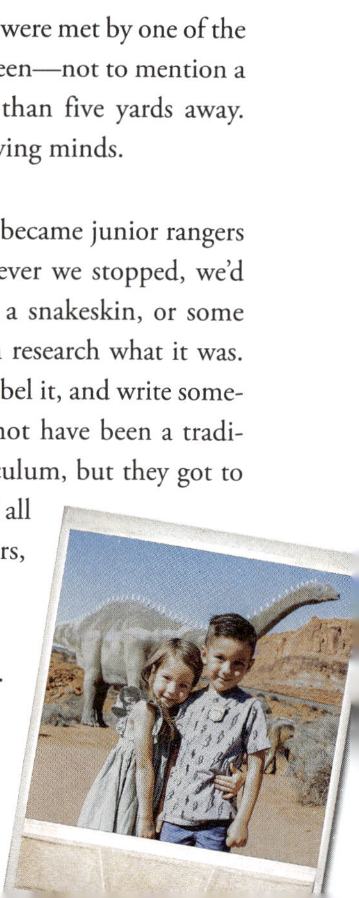

D: They also learned how to be brave and try new things. When we were in Utah, we went on a day hike in the desert.

Canyon was climbing on top of all these massive boulders like they were nothing. That kid used to battle a lot of fears, but after a few weeks on the road, he was running ahead of us on trails, climbing, swimming, and doing all kinds of things he'd never done before.

The same was true for Ember. There's a rope swing at the lake near my parents' house in Wisconsin, and before our trip, both of them would have been terrified to try something like that. But after our RV adventure, they were begging us to let them swing on it. Had we stayed home, they probably would have just hung out in the backyard and played in the house. This trip exposed them to a ton of different places and experiences that they're still talking about years later.

S: There's something about breaking away from your usual routine and trying something new that breathes fresh life into you. Not only do you discover new places and new things, but you also learn a lot about yourself. I never would have imagined myself behind the wheel of a thirty-five-foot RV!

D: Babe, it was two minutes.

S: I know, but I still did it—even though I was terrified and had no idea what I was doing.

D: Honestly, we were winging it for most of 2019 to 2022. Aside from the occasional social media slipup, bad investment, and broken tree limb, everything turned out just fine—better than fine, in fact—because we didn't give up.

S: A few years ago, Dan and I read a great book by John Maxwell called *Failing Forward.* In it he says that we should "fail early, fail often, but always fail forward." He defines failing forward as "the ability to get back up after you've been knocked down, learn from your mistake, and move forward in a better direction."

D: That's why we can't be afraid of making mistakes. A lot of times, our greatest mistakes can lead to our greatest successes. We just have to keep trying—even when we're scared and have no idea what we're doing. Because we never know what extraordinary experience God has waiting for us around the next corner.

Speaking of which . . . about midway through our trip, after driving all day, we arrived in Yellowstone National Park in the middle of the night. The kids were both sound asleep, so after finding a spot to camp for the evening, Sam and I walked to the back of the RV, climbed up the little ladder onto the roof, lay down, and just looked up at the stars. We had no agenda. There was no place we had to be and nobody we had to answer to.

We were just winging it. And it was one of the greatest adventures we've ever had.

DON'T LET NOT KNOWING

WHAT YOU ARE DOING STOP YOU FROM

Trying New Things.

PART OF CHOOSING ADVENTURE

IS BEING WILLING TO

Go With the Flow

AND FIGURE THINGS OUT AS YOU GO.

SEPTEMBER 2020
25 MILES NORTHEAST OF MULESHOE, COLORADO

D: As we pulled out of the parking lot, I turned and took one last look at Sam. Sitting there in the front seat of our broken-down loaner truck clutching a glorified starter pistol in her hand, she looked absolutely terrified. Just before a cloud of dust kicked up by Jerry's tires obscured my view, she shook her head and mouthed the words *I love you*. Or it might have been, *I'm so done with you*. It was kinda hard to tell.

I carefully positioned myself in the center of the back seat so I could have a clear view of where we were going. I figured if things got dicey and I had to tuck and roll, at least I'd have a chance at finding my way back to Sam. I also wanted to have a clear view of Fatty's and Jerry's hands. Sure, they *seemed* legit, but now they knew I had at least one credit card on me, and with acres of desert around us, it wouldn't be hard to hide a body.

We weren't on the road for two minutes when Jerry caught my eye in the rearview mirror. He smiled and said, "So . . . I guess we weren't quite what you were expecting."

Honestly, they weren't, but I sure as heck wasn't going to say anything to set them off. "How so?" I asked innocently.

He laughed and held out his right arm, exposing his scars, and rested his hand on Fatty's shoulder. "I mean, I'm all covered in burns, and my nephew here looks like he just got out of prison."

I laughed uncomfortably. Then I caught Fatty's eye in the reflection of the passenger side window and stopped. Dude looked dead serious.

Jerry glanced back at me and laughed again. "It's okay. I promise he's a good guy. He used to get in a lot of trouble back in the day, but now he works with underprivileged youth in our community. Helps them get out of gangs and off drugs and stuff like that."

"Whoa . . . cool," I said, trying not to look as surprised as I felt. When Fatty didn't say anything, I quickly turned back to Jerry, nodded at his arm, and said, "So how did you burn your arms?"

He shrugged. "A few years ago, my neighbor's house caught on fire in the middle of the night, and without thinking, I just ran in to get them out. I had to. Their kids were in there too."

I all but did a spit take. "Holy cow! Did everyone get out in time?"

"Oh yeah," he said. "I got burned pretty bad, though. Hurt like crazy when it happened." He held out his right hand and tried to clench his fingers. "Still have a hard time gripping stuff with this hand. That's why I asked Fatty here to come along with me. Tensioner pulleys can be a real bear to jimmy loose."

I felt terrible. I had completely misjudged these guys.

"So where are you two headed?" Jerry asked.

"Alamosa."

He nodded. "Have you had that truck long?"

I shook my head. "Just since this morning."

They glanced at each other, and Jerry's eyes narrowed. "You just bought it today?"

"Oh, it's not ours. Our vehicle broke down in Kansas, so a couple loaned us this one."

Jerry nodded. "Friends of yours?"

I shook my head. "Nope. Never met them before."

"And they just . . . *gave* it to you?" he asked.

I had to admit, it did sound a little sketchy. "Well . . . they loaned it to us." Now it sounded illegal.

They exchanged looks again, and Jerry shifted uncomfortably in his seat. I thought, *Great, here these two guys are saving people from burning buildings and getting kids off drugs, and now they think Sam and I stole a truck.* I had to say something.

"It's kind of a long story. My wife and I are from Missouri. We're on our way to Alamosa to compete in a reality show about renovating old buses and RVs, and as we were driving through Kansas this morning, my wife went to pass a semi. As soon as she started to accelerate, there was this loud clunking noise, and our vehicle started losing power. So we pulled off to the side of the road."

“Was there any smoke coming out?” Jerry asked.

“Nope. But when we started it up again, it made a grinding noise. So we called AAA, and while we were on hold, an older couple pulled up in a red Mustang and asked if we needed any help. By this point, I realized we were out of oil, so the guy says, ‘Tell you what. What if my wife stays here with your wife, and I take you to a gas station to pick up some oil?’”

“That was nice of him,” said Jerry.

“You don’t know the half of it. The guy’s wife got out and waited in our car with Sam while we picked up a quart of oil. When we came back and put the oil in, Sam tried the ignition, and it just started clanging.”

“That’s not good,” Fatty said with a chuckle.

“By that point, we’d been waiting for the tow truck from AAA for over an hour, so the guy said, ‘This might sound crazy—and you can totally say no—but we have an extra farm truck at our house. Why don’t you two come home with us and have some lunch, and then you can take our truck to Colorado, do your event, and just drop it off on your way back home.’”

Jerry looked stunned. “Are you serious?”

“Yeah. He’s going to take our vehicle to his mechanic on Monday and see if he can fix it.”

Fatty just shook his head. “Man, that’s wild.”

“I know!” I laughed. “Sam was so blown away, she burst into tears. It turns out they have a couple of kids our age, and they said that if this had happened to *their* kids, they hoped someone else would do the same.”

Jerry just smiled. “There are some good people out there.”

The dude was right. Fortunately for Sam and me, we had run into a bunch of them today.

From the second we set foot in the auto parts store, it was obvious that Jerry was basically a celebrity around there. It was also obvious that whoever answered the phone when I called had told pretty much everyone in the store about the guy from out of town whose truck had blown its tensioner pulley. I had barely made it through the front door when one of the locals leaning up against the counter smiled and said, “So you’re the guy who broke down out on Fifth Street.”

“Yep, I’m the guy.”

"You sure got lucky," he said, nodding in Jerry's direction. "There's not much Jerry here can't fix."

"I don't know that I'd call the day we've had *lucky*," I hedged. "But there's no question, someone has been looking out for us."

Before I could say anything further, Jerry appeared at my side with a new serpentine belt, a tensioner pulley, and a gallon of engine coolant. "I had a feeling we'd need all these," he said, "so I had them pull them for me ahead of time."

Wow, I thought, *he is good.* I had completely forgotten about the coolant. I handed the cashier my credit card and watched him ring up roughly one hundred dollars' worth of parts. As we headed out to the truck, Jerry stopped for a second, then asked, "You have tools with you in that truck?"

"Yeah," I said. Conveniently, we had brought most of my power tools with us to use on the show. "Why, what do you need?"

"You wouldn't happen to have a longer wrench?"

"No, I don't. Do we need one?"

He nodded. "Tensioner pulleys are really hard to loosen," he said, hopping in the truck. "It's okay—we can swing by my house and pick one up."

As we pulled out of the parking lot and onto the main road, going in the opposite direction we'd come from, I started to get a little nervous about the time. It was starting to get dark, Alamosa was still several hours away, and I had no idea how long it would take to change the pulley and belt.

"Do you live far?" I asked.

"Just a few miles off the main drag," he said, pulling off the highway and onto a single-lane dirt road.

About ten minutes later, we pulled up a long driveway that led to a small house in the middle of nowhere.

"I'll be right back," Jerry said, jumping out of the truck, followed closely by Fatty.

As I sat there by myself in the truck, all I could think was, *Man, Sam's mom would have a field day with this.* She'd texted Sam twice when we broke down in Kansas. Sam finally texted her back:

> Hey, long story short. Car died on the side of the road. A couple stopped. I promise they're safe. Their names are Greg and Andrea. We're on the way to their house. They have an extra car we can use. I'll keep you updated . . .

When Sam's mom got this text, she lost her ever-loving mind.

That, of course, prompted her to call Sam. And when Sam didn't answer she called Sam again and then called me twice. Sam eventually texted her:

I promise we're OK.

Robin texted back:

Get a picture of their license plate!

I swear, I thought to myself, *that woman flies into a panic faster than—* That's when it hit me. "Oh, crap!" I immediately reached for my phone. As expected, there were about a half dozen texts and missed calls, all from Sam. I completely forgot that I'd set my phone on silent after we left Greg and Andrea's house that afternoon. I always do that when I'm driving someplace unfamiliar so I won't get distracted. And since I was driving their truck, I wanted to make sure I could focus.

Just as I started to text her back, someone knocked on the window, and I all but jumped out of my own skin.

"Hello!" It was a short, heavyset Hispanic woman. She looked to be in her mid-fifties and had long dark hair streaked with gray pulled back from her face in a bun. She wore a smile a mile wide and was carrying a large serving platter piled high with steaming tamales.

I stopped texting and rolled the window down. "Hello."

Her English was limited, but based on what I could remember from high school Spanish, she seemed to be saying that she was Jerry's wife.

"Are you hungry?" she asked, holding up the tray of tamales.

"Oh, no," I said, politely. "But thank you very much."

"Are you sure?" she tried again. They looked and smelled fantastic.

"I'm positive," I assured her. She looked a little disappointed, but not nearly as disappointed as Sam would be if she ever found out that while she was clinging to a BB gun in the middle of nowhere, convinced I was dead, I was enjoying a plate of tamales.

Fortunately, Fatty and Jerry emerged from the house, and she turned her attention to them, giving me a chance to finish my text to Sam.

I'm OK. Got the parts. Had to go to Jerry's house to get a bigger wrench. Will be back soon.

I knew she was going to be ticked. I mean, dang, I'd even promised to keep my phone on. Figuring I'd hear about it when we got back—and possibly for the rest of my life—I put my phone in my pocket just as Jerry and Fatty got back into the truck.

"Okay," Jerry said, firing up the engine. "Let's get you two back on the road."

Twenty minutes later, we were back at the scene of the crime. The second I saw Sam's face, I knew I was in trouble.

She came out of the truck to meet us, and before she could say a word, I said, "I know. I forgot my phone was off, and I'm so sorry. But babe, I'm telling you, these guys are saints. I'll explain later."

Fatty and Jerry spent the next twenty minutes working like crazy, elbow deep in the engine, with only a tiny magnetic light stuck to the bottom of the hood to see by. As I stood watching them, two things became abundantly clear: one, even if I'd gotten the part, there was no way I would have been able to fix that truck myself—not without that wrench and a second set of hands. Two, Sam and I were undoubtedly two of the most blessed individuals on the planet.

"Okay," Jerry said, surveying his work. "Go ahead and fire it up."

I said a quick prayer, then turned the key in the ignition. Wouldn't you know it, that engine purred like a kitten.

Jerry gave me a thumbs-up over the hood. "Sounds good," he called out. "Let it run for a little bit. Let's make sure everything is okay before you head back out."

We let it run for about five more minutes, during which time Fatty and Jerry double-checked all the fluids, belts, and gauges, and I told Sam about Jerry's burns, Fatty's volunteer work, and the tamales I'd graciously turned down. For the second time that day, Sam was so overwhelmed with gratitude that she almost started to cry.

Finally satisfied, Jerry slammed the hood down. "Okay, you're all good to go."

Sam grabbed my arm and whispered, "We have to give them something."

"All I have is a twenty," I whispered back. We both knew that wasn't nearly enough.

"Listen," I said, "I only have twenty dollars on me, but if you follow us, we can go to a gas station or something. I'm sure they'll have an ATM."

Jerry held up his hand and said, "Don't worry about it. We're good."

"No, please," Sam said. "We have to give you something. You came all this way, and—"

"Please," Jerry interrupted. "It's okay. You just get to Alamosa safely."

We were floored. They wouldn't even accept the cash I had with me. They just waved goodbye, got in their truck, and drove away.

Then Sam and I got back in Greg and Andrea's truck, I turned the key, and once again, it started right up. In fact, if I didn't know better, I'd swear it sounded better than it had all day. I looked at Sam, shook my head, and laughed. "Can you believe those guys?"

She shook her head back. "Seriously."

We pulled out onto the highway, and a few hours later, we arrived in Alamosa. By the time we arrived at the event site, we were both exhausted. I turned off the engine and looked at Sam, who for the past twenty minutes or so had been silently staring out the passenger-side window.

"You okay, babe?"

"Yeah," she said, still looking off into the distance. "I was just thinking . . . you know how the Bible says we should always be kind to strangers because you never know when they might be angels in disguise?"

"Yeah?"

She turned to me and, with a playful smile, said, "Is it weird that I kinda wanna call that O'Reilly store back and ask if they even know a Jerry and a Fatty?"

For the record, we didn't.

Also for the record? It wouldn't have surprised us one bit if they'd said no.

10

SO...
Now What?

D: So what's next for us?

S: We're excited about what lies ahead. But we're willing to bet it's not at all what you're expecting. Are you ready?

D: Wait for it . . .

S: We've decided to settle down. That's right—after almost a decade of constantly being on the move, living in RVs, and staying with family and friends, we have officially become homeowners.

D: It's funny . . . for the longest time, we thought putting down roots was a bad thing, but we're really excited about the idea of sitting still for a while—not in a "we're never going to leave the house again" kind of way, but in a "let's establish a home base where we can share exciting new experiences with the people we love" kind of way.

S: Maybe it's a result of having spent so much time on our own, but for the past year or so, we've found ourselves craving community—not only for us, but for our kids as well.

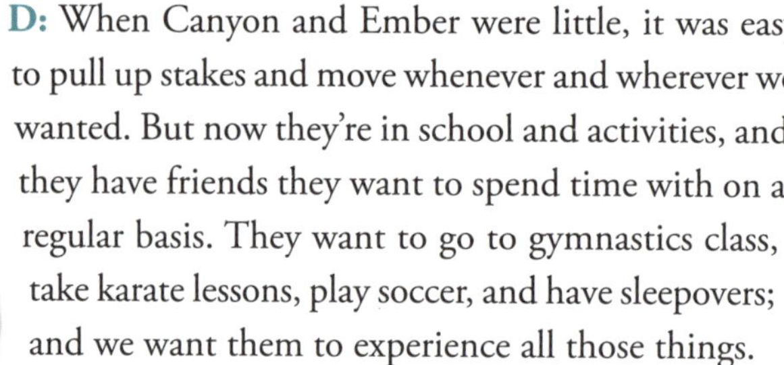

D: When Canyon and Ember were little, it was easy to pull up stakes and move whenever and wherever we wanted. But now they're in school and activities, and they have friends they want to spend time with on a regular basis. They want to go to gymnastics class, take karate lessons, play soccer, and have sleepovers; and we want them to experience all those things.

S: What's more, we want to experience those things with them. We've spent so many years helping other couples start their families, and now that our kids are getting older, we want to make the most of every minute we have with them.

D: Plus, after living "small" for so many years, we're excited to finally have a little extra space—not so we can fill it with stuff but so we can fill it with people. We want to be a landing spot for family and friends who need a place to stay during their own travels and adventures, the same way our friends in Alaska, Sam's relatives out West, and my family up north have been for us.

S: Shortly after hitting the road full-time in the RV, we realized we were missing community. Don't get me wrong, we made a ton of memories on the road with our family of four, but we missed making memories with others too. Our home now allows us to do that. We are excited about hosting gatherings—barbecues, game nights, movie nights, cooking clubs, and Bible studies—and creating a space where people can relax, have fun, grow in faith, and create lifelong friendships and memories.

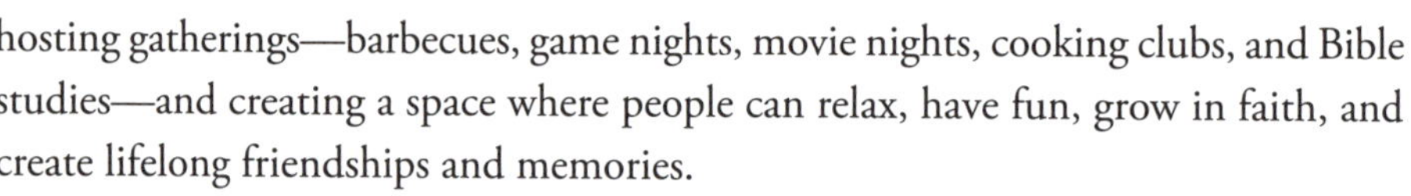

D: But just because we're settling down doesn't mean we're "settling." Travel and adventure will always be a huge part of our lives. Sometime in the next year, we plan to go back out West and take the kids four-wheeling in Utah. We want to go back to Yosemite and Yellowstone, and maybe even visit the Canadian side of Glacier National Park. Heck, I'd love to drive all the way across Canada.

S: And of course, we still plan to make our annual treks down to Florida.

D: Actually, now that I think about it, the kids have never been to the Grand Canyon.

S: Or Niagara Falls.

D: You know, I wasn't going to say anything, but when I was double-checking the specs of the motor home for the previous chapter, I realized how much I miss it. I mean, I could do without driving through construction, but that view of the Badlands . . .

S: Wait . . . are you serious?

D: Kinda . . . yeah.

S: Oh my gosh, we should totally get a Class C motor home. Those are so much smaller—I could even help you drive. I bet I could find a used one on Facebook Marketplace that we could fix up real cute, and—

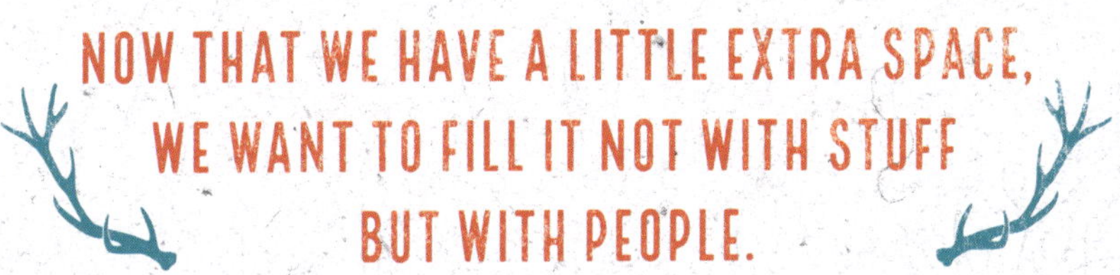

D: See? We're still Dan and Sam. We just have a more permanent address.

S: And a garage, babe. And you know what that means . . .

D: Yep. I'm gettin' a canoe.

D: By the way, in case you were wondering, we won the *Gutted* competition. And our vehicle? The one that broke down back in Kansas? Yeah, it was pretty much totaled.

Sam and I used our prize money to rent a Yukon to get us back to Missouri. Along the way, we dropped the farm truck back off at Greg and Andrea's house. Thanks to Fatty and Jerry, it ran beautifully. We made a gift of the new serpentine belt and tensioner pulley and left our old vehicle and title with Greg and Andrea to sell for us. We knew it probably wasn't worth much, but we offered to let them keep whatever they got for it. They refused. (We still think they might be angels also.)

From a financial standpoint, the whole trip was pretty much a wash. We lost our vehicle, and the little money we won barely covered our expenses. But we had a great time, and we met a bunch of amazing people—some of whom we're still friends with today. At the end of the day, that's all we really cared about. The fact that we won was just icing on the cake.

The weird thing was, normally, Sam and I are the most adventurous people in the group, but once we got to Alamosa, we were by far the most conventional people there. All the other competitors lived in their converted buses, RVs, or vans full-time and had for years. Because the van community is so close, we were pretty much outsiders, and there was a lot we didn't know.

For one thing, all the RVs we'd worked on already had their own plumbing and HVAC systems, but it turns out vans only have an exhaust fan to circulate fresh air.

If you have to go . . . well, you have to step outside. I gotta admit, it's not often Sam and I are the "bougie" members of any group, but in this crowd, just having a toilet and running water catapulted us into elite status. Even though we didn't know anything about diesel heaters or portable dry-flush toilets (which are actually pretty cool), we *did* have a lot of experience renovating vehicles and making them not only livable but beautiful.

Sam has always had a great eye for design, which she brought to the table big-time—especially in regard to picking out bedding, decor, and other personal touches that made our vehicle look far more finished than the bus or even the RV.

S: And Dan was probably the most experienced carpenter on the team, so in addition to helping with the flooring, he did a lot of custom woodwork, including these really cool windowsills that doubled as shelves.

D: As for the rest of the team, Jarrod knew a lot about electrical stuff and came up with a really cool idea for installing indirect lighting in the ceiling.

S: And Stephi was an amazing artist. She painted these awesome nature scenes on the walls inside the van and an absolutely spectacular mural on the hood.

WHEN WE GIVE OUR DECISIONS OVER TO GOD,
WAIT TO FEEL HIS PEACE,
AND THEN STEP FORWARD IN FAITH,
GOOD THINGS SEEM TO FOLLOW.

THE POINT ISN'T TO FOLLOW OUR PATH— IT'S TO DISCOVER YOUR OWN.

D: Nick was a certified marine electrician and the mastermind behind the van's HVAC system, and Brandon was a jack-of-all-trades. There was literally nothing that guy couldn't do.

S: Then there was Linnea—we love Linnea. She's the kind of free spirit who makes Dan and me look like a couple of uptight yuppies. She lives in the desert for months at a time with her dog, with no electricity, no cell service—nothing. She's incredibly sweet and gentle, but she's also really tough. She taught me how to cut through the metal ceiling with a jigsaw so we could install the exhaust fan.

D: We were definitely an eclectic team. Everyone brought their own unique skills and talents to the table, and we worked well together. In fact, we managed to do in just five days what would normally take upwards of six months.

S: Plus, it was fun to spend a week with people who lived the kind of nomadic, minimalist lifestyle we wanted for ourselves. Come to think of it, that was right around the time I started emailing Camping World, so had it not been for *Gutted*, we might have missed out on one of our greatest adventures.

D: In a lot of ways, *Gutted* was the greatest adventure we've ever had—not because we won the competition but because of everything we went through to get there. It's like Clark Griswold said at the beginning of *National Lampoon's Vacation*, "Getting there is half the fun."

S: Yeah, I don't know that I'd call breaking down on the side of the road twice or worrying that you'd been kidnapped by two ex-felons *fun*, but it definitely affirmed our belief that no matter what happens, as long as we put our trust in the Lord and follow his lead, he *will* provide.

We saw his provision through Greg and Andrea, who looked at us, saw their own kids, and knew they had to help, and in Fatty and Jerry, who graciously gave up their time without asking for anything in return.

D: We even saw it in the rest of our *Gutted* team, who came out to the desert hoping to win a competition only to get saddled with a couple of outsiders who didn't know a thing about vans. Yet they instantly embraced us, trusted us to get the job done, and taught us some new skills.

S: We get that a lot of people might look at that story and say, "Man, check out all the stuff that went wrong." But when we look back on it, all we see is the stuff that went right.

D: A lot of people might see our adventures and say, "Wow, you guys have really gotten lucky." But you know what? I don't believe in luck. I believe in divine intervention. When we give our decisions over to God, wait to feel his peace, and then step forward in faith, good things seem to follow. We've experienced it far too often to see it any other way.

S: That said, we know the Lord has poured far more blessings on us than we deserve. We also know that our approach to living isn't for everyone—and that's okay. You don't have to do what we did. Heck, if we had to do it all over again, even *we* probably wouldn't do everything we did.

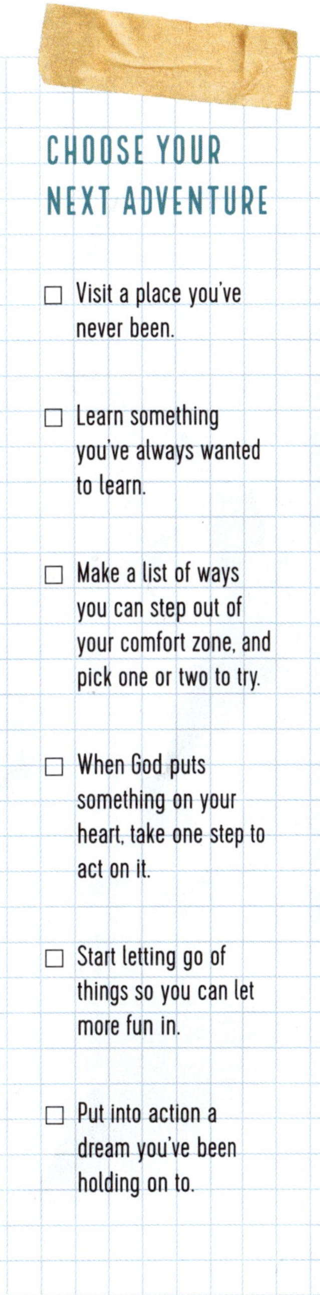

CHOOSE YOUR NEXT ADVENTURE

- ☐ Visit a place you've never been.
- ☐ Learn something you've always wanted to learn.
- ☐ Make a list of ways you can step out of your comfort zone, and pick one or two to try.
- ☐ When God puts something on your heart, take one step to act on it.
- ☐ Start letting go of things so you can let more fun in.
- ☐ Put into action a dream you've been holding on to.

D: The point isn't to follow our path—it's to discover your own. That's what choosing adventure is all about. So what are you waiting for?

> Step out of your comfort zone.
> Go someplace you've never been.
> Try something you've never done.
> Give God a chance to show up in your life.
> And when he does, get ready for the adventure of a lifetime.
> But whatever you do, don't let fear get in the way of living your best life.
> Take a leap of faith.
> *What's the worst that could happen?*

DON'T LET FEAR

GET IN THE WAY OF LIVING

Your Best Life.

Surrogacy FAQs

We get a lot of questions about surrogacy on social media and in real life. These questions come from people who are interested in becoming surrogates, people who want to connect with a surrogate, and people who simply want to know more about the process. Here are a few of the topics that commonly come up:

What's the difference between traditional surrogacy and gestational surrogacy?

In traditional surrogacy, the surrogate's eggs are used, so she is biologically related to the baby. In gestational surrogacy, the surrogate has no biological link to the baby. She just provides the womb.

What does *IP(s)* stand for?

IP(s) refers to "intended parent(s)"—an individual or couple who is hoping to build their family through surrogacy.

On average, what base compensation do surrogates receive?

Surrogate compensation is not a set number, but an average compensation for a first-time surrogate is around $30,000 to $60,000. Many factors play into this. Does the surrogate have surrogacy-friendly insurance? Have they done a surrogacy journey before? Do they live close to or far from the IPs? All these factors affect a surrogate's compensation and can justify a higher or lower comp. Ultimately, it's up to the IPs to determine what they're willing to compensate a surrogate or what a surrogate thinks a journey is worth for her time and commitment, as well as the physical toll on her body.

We hope this goes without saying, but we don't think anyone should explore surrogacy *for the sake of* compensation. In fact, one of the requirements of becoming a surrogate is that you are not on state insurance, meaning you should be able to fully support yourself and your family before being compensated. Life is sacred, and no amount of money can equal the gift of a child or fully cover the spiritual, physical, and mental toll this journey can take. Rather, compensation is intended to help make surrogacy possible for a woman when it might not otherwise be. In our case, we were compensated for our first surrogacy journey. On our second journey, we decided to forgo compensation, telling our intended parents we wanted them to use the money for their growing family.

How long does a surrogacy journey last, from start to finish?

Most journeys take at least a year, including being matched with IPs, getting medical clearance, finalizing the contract, doing the medication protocols and the transfer, and going through the pregnancy and delivery. Some journeys can be two years plus if the matching process takes longer or if multiple transfers are needed.

What's the difference between an open and a closed relationship?

An open relationship means the surrogate and the IPs stay in touch after the journey is over. A closed relationship means there is no contact after the journey is complete. It's important to make sure the surrogate and the IPs are on the same page when they begin a journey.

How do you handle postpartum as a surrogate?

Going into a journey, you know that the baby you're carrying is not for you to keep and care for, which makes the postpartum journey easier. I focused on my own family, things I loved to do, and the Lord as I walked through postpartum. This helped me be happy and at peace with what I was able to do for someone else.

How do you explain surrogacy to your children?

When explaining surrogacy to our children, we always said, "Wouldn't it be nice for Mommy to help someone else have a baby?" We never called the baby *brother* or *sister*. They always knew the baby in my belly was for someone else.

What are the requirements to become a surrogate?

- Have at least one previous successful pregnancy and no more than five vaginal births or three cesarean deliveries.
- Be currently raising your child(ren).
- Have no major complications from previous pregnancies.
- Be between the ages of twenty-one and forty-five (though age requirements may vary depending on health).
- Have a BMI of 30 or less.
- No smoking or use of illegal drugs.
- Have a good support system and be financially stable, without reliance on government aid.
- Have no felony convictions.
- Be off all mental-health medications for at least twelve months prior to starting a surrogacy journey and be feeling good without meds.
- Be able to travel as needed for appointments. Depending on who you are matched with, you may need to travel by plane or car at least twice.

Do you have to eat a certain diet?

Most of the time, there aren't diet restrictions, but sometimes the IPs want their surrogate to be on a certain diet. In these cases, there may be higher compensation or a higher monthly allowance.

How does delivery go as a surrogate?

The surrogate decides how she wants to deliver under the advice of her ob-gyn, but it's nice to consider the desires of the IPs as well. Most of the time, the IPs are in the delivery room, but the surrogate decides what she is most comfortable with. It's best if the surrogate and the IPs decide on a birth plan together—something both parties feel at peace with.

What is the process for becoming a surrogate?

- *Matching:* This process includes making sure your support person is on board, deciding what you want out of the journey, and ultimately getting paired with IPs whose beliefs and desires align with yours. This can be done independently or through an agency.
- *Medical examination:* You will be required to meet with a fertility specialist for a physical exam and blood work to ensure your suitability for surrogacy. The doctor will go over your former pregnancy or pregnancies and delivery records during this meeting and explain what you can expect from the embryo transfer and the rest of the process.
- *Mental health evaluation:* You will meet with a mental health professional (most likely over video chat) to ensure that you understand the emotional impact of surrogacy and are psychologically ready for the challenges of surrogate motherhood.
- *Medical screening:* This part of the screening process involves a physical exam as well as a variety of laboratory tests. You will be screened for sexually transmitted diseases and other communicable diseases, as well as certain viruses and infections that can affect your fertility. You may need to undergo an ultrasound to determine the health of your uterus, and you might be screened for drug use. Your spouse or partner will likely also need to be screened for STDs and drug use.
- *Legal:* You and the IPs will both have attorneys, and you will sign contracts. It is also wise to have a trusted escrow company handle the finances for the journey.

- *Fertility treatments:* After signing legal contracts with the IPs, you will need to prepare for surrogate pregnancy with fertility treatments, blood tests, injections, and ultrasounds throughout the embryo transfer process (as well as in the beginning of your pregnancy). You will be prescribed several medications, including hormones such as estrogen and progesterone to help regulate your cycle and prepare you for in vitro fertilization (IVF).
- *Embryo transfer:* If the IPs already have embryos, you will begin with the transfer. If not, the intended mother's egg (or the donor's egg) will be fertilized in the laboratory using the intended father's sperm (or the donor's sperm). After a brief incubation period, the fertilized embryo will be transferred into your uterus for implantation. This procedure is relatively quick and painless and usually doesn't require medication or anesthesia.
- *Prenatal care:* You will be required to make routine visits to the fertility clinic to receive regular blood tests and ultrasounds. Once a heartbeat is heard and a healthy pregnancy is confirmed, you may be transferred to your own OB. You will continue to receive prenatal care as you would with any pregnancy, though checkups may be more frequent to ensure the health of the baby. The IPs come to you when it's time for the delivery, and they usually stay at an Airbnb or a hotel near the hospital.

Acknowledgments

To our kids: Every day with you both is an adventure. We are beyond blessed to be your parents and to raise you up in the ways of the Lord. We pray that throughout your lives, you will continue to seek God and choose adventure.

To our parents: Thank you for adventuring with us when we were young. Thank you for the sacrifices you made to prioritize quality time as a family. Those memories drive us to do the same with our children today.

To our friends: Thank you for being by our side throughout our highs and lows and for allowing us to live in your basement and run businesses out of your garage, for keeping us grounded, and for coming on some of these crazy adventures with us.

To Kirk Noonan: Thank you for all your wisdom and insight through the early years of our marriage. Your encouragement to take the most adventurous route in life was the launchpad for the life we're now living.

To our followers: Thank you for your support and encouragement over the years. The friendships we've made online have motivated us to continue to share our lives and adventures with you all. We couldn't do it without you.

To God: We are blown away by your continued faithfulness and provision. The blessings we've received are more than we could ever ask for. Thank you for allowing us to be a vessel to share your love with others. You will always be the center of our adventures, and we can't wait to see what you have in store for us next.

Notes

SEPTEMBER 2020, 25 MILES NORTHEAST OF MULESHOE, COLORADO

"'I'm just saying, Samantha, according to this website, there is a crime committed in Alamosa every five hours . . .'"
"The Safest and Most Dangerous Places in Alamosa, CO: Crime Maps and Statistics," CrimeGrade.org, accessed October 4, 2024, https://crimegrade.org/safest-places-in-alamosa-co.

DON'T WAIT FOR THE PERFECT MOMENT

"'It's not good for the Man to be alone; I'll make him a helper, a companion.'"
Genesis 2:18, MSG.
"There's even evidence that maintaining healthy relationships can strengthen our immune systems, . . ."
"Strong Relationships, Strong Health," Better Health Channel, accessed October 7, 2024, https://www.betterhealth.vic.gov.au/health/healthyliving/Strong-relationships-strong-health.
"Like Franklin D. Roosevelt said, 'The only thing we have to fear is fear itself.'"
"Franklin D. Roosevelt," The White House, accessed October 7, 2024, https://www.whitehouse.gov/about-the-white-house/presidents/franklin-d-roosevelt.
2 Timothy 1:7 is taken from the NLT.
"Actually, that reminds me, there's an awesome episode of The Big Bang Theory *. . ."*
The Big Bang Theory, season 7, episode 19, "The Indecision Amalgamation," directed by Anthony Rich, written by Chuck Lorre, Bill Prady, and Steven Molaro, featuring Johnny Galecki, Jim Parsons, and Kaley Cuoco, aired April 3, 2014.

JUST WHEN YOU THOUGHT YOUR LIFE WAS OVER

"Generally speaking, most experts agree that the best thing we can do for our kids is to maintain a happy, healthy marriage."
Debbie L. Cherry, "How Taking Care of Your Marriage Is the Best Thing for Your Kids," Focus on the Family Canada, accessed October 7, 2024, https://www.focusonthefamily.ca/content/how-taking-care-of-your-marriage-is-the-best-thing-for-your-kids.

GOING THOUGH BROKE

"The best way I can explain it is with a story from the Gospel of Matthew. . . ."
See Matthew 14:22-33.

"Take Abraham, for example. One day God told him, 'Take your son, your only son, . . .'"
See Genesis 22.
"Psalm 139 tells us, 'God . . . I'm an open book to you; . . .'"
Psalm 139:1-12, MSG.

KEEP MOVING FORWARD

"Bear Grylls, one of the greatest adventurers of all time, once said, 'Whenever you do something . . .'"
Bear Grylls, *A Survival Guide for Life: How to Achieve Your Goals, Thrive in Adversity, and Grow in Character* (London: Bantam Press, 2012), 219. Italics in original.
"But as Pastor Rick Warren writes, 'Fear is always worse than reality. . . .'"
Rick Warren, "Two Ways to Tackle Fear," PastorRick.com, June 18, 2019, https://pastorrick.com/two-ways-to-tackle-fear.
"I think it's fitting that Psalm 119 calls God's Word 'a lamp *. . .'"*
Psalm 119:105, NLT, italics added.
"There's a great story in the Gospel of Matthew that sums this up beautifully. . . ."
See Matthew 25:14-30, MSG.
"In the Gospel of Luke, Jesus tells his disciples, 'Do not worry . . .'"
Luke 12:22-25.
". . . we can do what God tells us to do and cast all our anxiety on him."
See 1 Peter 5:7.
"I think Bear Grylls was spot-on when he said, 'Adventure should be 80 percent . . .'"
"Life Lessons from Bear Grylls," Advance Performance, accessed October 11, 2024, https://www.advance-performance.co.uk/blog-leadership/life-lessons-bear-grylls.

THERE HAS TO BE MORE TO LIFE

"Brian Dyson, the former CEO of Coca-Cola made a great analogy. . . ."
Brian G. Dyson, from Georgia Tech Institute's 172nd commencement address, September 6, 1991. See Rabieh Adib, "Five Balls of Life: Coca-Cola's Former CEO Brian Dyson's Commencement Speech on Love, Work, Family and Friendship," Shine Coaching, October 23, 2024, https://www.shinecoachingbarcelona.com/en/5-balls-of-life-brian-dyson-speech.
"As bestselling author Stephen Covey wrote, 'The key is . . .'"
Stephen R. Covey, *The Seven Habits of Highly Effective People* (New York: Free Press, 2004), 161.

THE PATH LESS TRAVELED

"In case you're wondering, traditional surrogacy is when the surrogate's eggs are used, . . ."
"About Surrogacy: Traditional vs. Gestational Surrogacy—What's Best for My Family?" Surrogate.com, accessed October 11, 2024, https://surrogate.com/about-surrogacy/types-of-surrogacy/traditional-vs-gestational-surrogacy-whats-best-for-my-family.
"Then I looked at what would be required of me as a surrogate. . . ."
"Surrogates: How Can I Become a Surrogate?" Surrogate.com, accessed October 11, 2024, https://surrogate.com/surrogates/becoming-a-surrogate/how-can-i-become-a-surrogate-mother.
Psalm 37:5 is taken from the NLT.
"'It is more blessed to give than to receive.'"
Acts 20:35.

LEAVING IT ALL BEHIND

"There's a great scene in Mel Brooks's classic Star Wars *spoof,* Spaceballs, *. . ."*
Mel Brooks, dir., *Spaceballs* (Beverly Hills, CA: Metro-Goldwyn-Mayer, 1987). See video clip at Serse1000, "Spaceballs Hair Dryer Scene," YouTube, posted August 9, 2009, https://www.youtube.com/watch?v=G1CYg0vIygE.

"As of 2024, the US self-storage business has mushroomed . . ."
Al Harris, "U.S. Self-Storage Industry Statistics," SpareFoot, updated August 1, 2024, https://www.sparefoot.com/self-storage/news/1432-self-storage-industry-statistics.

"According to bestselling author and professional tidying expert (because apparently that's a thing) Marie Kondo, . . ."
Marie Kondo, *The Life-Changing Magic of Tidying Up: The Japanese Art of Decluttering and Organizing* (Berkeley: Ten Speed Press, 2014), 181.

"Like the professional tidying expert says, 'Presents are not "things" . . .'"
Kondo, *The Life-Changing Magic*, 108.

"People were allegedly filling plastic bags with gasoline . . ."
Christopher Brito, "Officials Warn People Not to Fill Plastic Bags with Gasoline amid Panic over Gas Shortage," CBS News, May 14, 2021, https://www.cbsnews.com/news/gas-shortage-plastic-bags-warning-consumer-product-safety.

"Psychologists call it panic buying, and it's basically a coping mechanism . . ."
Kimberly Dawn Neumann, "The Psychology of Panic Buying," Forbes.com, updated January 27, 2023, https://www.forbes.com/health/mind/panic-buying.

Leviticus 25:20-21 is paraphrased.

". . . he told them not to bring anything with them other than a walking stick and the clothes on their backs."
See Mark 6:7-13.

SOMETIMES YOU JUST GOTTA WING IT

". . . 'influencer' was one of the most popular career aspirations for our generation."
"How the Influencer Dream Is Shaping Young People's Goals," Adobe Express, September 13, 2024, https://www.adobe.com/express/learn/blog/wanting-to-be-influencer.

". . . very few were making a successful living doing it."
Justin Moore, "How Much Money Do Instagram Influencers Make in 2021?," Creator Wizard, accessed October 16, 2024, https://www.creatorwizard.com/post/how-much-money-do-instagram-influencers-make-in-2021.

". . . he says that we should 'fail early, fail often, but always fail forward.'"
John C. Maxwell, *Failing Forward: Turning Mistakes into Stepping Stones for Success* (New York: HarperCollins, 2007), 203.

"He defines failing forward as 'the ability to get back up . . .'"
John Maxwell, *1000+ John C. Maxwell Quotes* (UB Tech, 2018), 54.

SEPTEMBER 2020, 25 MILES NORTHEAST OF MULESHOE, COLORADO

"'. . . you know how the Bible says we should always be kind to strangers . . .'"
See Hebrews 13:2.

SO . . . NOW WHAT?

"It's like Clark Griswold said at the beginning of National Lampoon's Vacation, . . ."

Harold Ramis, dir., *National Lampoon's Vacation* (Burbank, CA: Warner Bros, 1983).

SURROGACY FAQS

"What's the difference between traditional surrogacy and gestational surrogacy? . . ."

"About Surrogacy: Traditional vs. Gestational Surrogacy—What's Best for My Family?" Surrogate.com, accessed October 11, 2024, https://surrogate.com/about-surrogacy/types-of-surrogacy/traditional-vs-gestational-surrogacy-whats-best-for-my-family.

"What are the requirements to become a surrogate? . . ."

"Surrogates: How Can I Become a Surrogate?" Surrogate.com, accessed October 11, 2024, https://surrogate.com/surrogates/becoming-a-surrogate/how-can-i-become-a-surrogate-mother.

"What is the process for becoming a surrogate? . . ."

"Surrogates: The Six Steps of the Surrogacy Process," Surrogate.com, accessed October 16, 2024, https://surrogate.com/surrogates/becoming-a-surrogate/the-six-steps-of-the-surrogacy-process/.

About the Authors

Dan and Sam Mathews have been married since 2014 and currently reside in Missouri with their two kids, Canyon and Ember. Since the moment they got married, Dan and Samantha have been living a life of sacrifice and faith. From backpacking in Arkansas to RV road trips across the US, they have always taken the adventurous route. Sam is a lifestyle vlogger and content creator, and Dan hosts a hunting podcast in addition to his social platforms. Together they share their life of adventure online with millions of followers.

DENALI
NATIONAL PARK
STOP
SCHOOL BUS
ALASKA
FLORIDA
MAP OF

GUTTED
WELCOME TO
COLORADO